PARISH LEADERSHIP

✦

Principles and Perspectives

✦

William J. Byron, S.J.

Published by:

Clear Faith Publishing LLC
22 Lafayette Rd
Princeton, NJ 08540

ISBN 978-1-940414-16-4

Printed in the United States of America

First Printing February, 2017
Cover and Interior Design by Doug Cordes
Parish Leadership is typeset in Linotype Gianotten and Cinta

Contact Information

261 City Ave.
Merion Station, PA 19066-1835
610-660-1424; wbyron@sju.edu

In appreciation of the work
Reverend J. Bryan Hehir
has done so admirably,
combining a commitment to
scholarship in Catholic Social Thought
with classroom teaching
and leadership service at the parish level

Table of Contents

Introduction

This book is intended primarily, but not exclusively, for Catholic pastors—i.e., for ordained men whose discipleship puts them on the path of sacramental service to a defined faith community. These are words of encouragement, not criticism, offered in admiration with an intention of being helpful. Not all ordained pastors measure up to the leadership responsibilities that are theirs; this book will help them recognize their missed leadership opportunities and encourage them to overcome their omissions. It will also, I hope, help them recognize the potential for revolutionary change that lies within their reach. To lead is to change, as the last chapter in this book explains. The what, when, where, and how of pastoral change is covered in these pages.

This book is also very much intended for non-ordained lay men and women whose vocation puts them on the path of pastoral service to the Catholic faith community. Parish leadership must be shared; otherwise it will surely fail. Here again the leadership challenge associated with this vocation is sometimes met and sometimes missed; the principles outlined in these pages can serve both to energize and renew parish life and pastoral service.

"Principle" is a word that registers on the ear with the exact same tone as the word "principal," but when these words meet the eye, they convey altogether distinct meanings. A principle—"ple"—l-e-a-d-s to something; it puts "legs" under one's values. Principles prompt action or serve to promote inaction in situations where to act would be to do something morally wrong. A "principled" person knows where he or she is coming from and where he or she is likely to end up. Principled and purposeful are twin characteristics of a mature person of character leading a responsible life.

Principles of parish leadership will be listed and explained throughout this book. They will be set forth clearly and succinctly for easy assimilation and understanding. The hope here is to bring providers of parish service—men and women, ordained and not ordained—together on a common ground of shared convictions capable of shaping a parish culture. That's what a culture is—a set of shared meanings and values. The meanings and values will be expressed here in principle form. Once understood and internalized by the parish team, the principles will energize the parish.

Interestingly enough, a team of individuals who, say, are the mainstays of a law firm or a financial services company are often called "principals." They are key leaders with separate responsibilities, but they all share the same principles. They are sometimes called partners, but, again, are united by shared principles. The partnership works best when the principals communicate among themselves and work together seamlessly. And so it goes at the leadership level of successful parishes.

Another way to view this book is to see it as a construction project. Chapter 1 provides a foundation for all that follows. I like to think of the first chapter as an infrastructure, a spirituality in which all the principles are grounded. The elements that constitute the infrastructure have to be shared by all members of the parish team if that team is to function effectively. And that raises the question of compatibility. Do all the members of the team belong there? If not, the team member who does not fit will have to change or move on. It is the pastor's job to form the team, to "massage" the members at the level of principle to make sure that compatibility reinforces the infrastructure. This will become clearer once I list the elements of the infrastructure; let me remark here, however, that they are all lifted from Scripture and thus should be available and congenial to all.

Although most of my working life has been spent in higher education, I had experience as a full-time pastor from 2000 to 2003 at Holy Trinity Catholic Church in the Georgetown section of Washington, DC. And for the past ten years I have been a weekend assistant at Annunciation Parish in Havertown, PA, a suburb of Philadelphia. Holy Trinity had 9,500 registered parishioners when I was there; about half of them came from Northern Virginia. We had a parish elementary school that was one of the best in the city, a parish council, a finance council, an active religious education program for youngsters enrolled in non-Catholic schools, an RCIA (Rite of Christian Initiation of Adults) program, and a year-round marriage preparation program offered in segments of six successive Thursday evening sessions several times a year. Let your Internet search engine take you to "Holy Trinity Catholic Church, Washington, DC" for an up-to-the-moment description of what is happening there.

Table imagery is helpful in gaining perspective on parish leadership. The Table of the Eucharist is at the center of it all; the regular weekly gatherings of parish staff around a meeting table in the parish center provide direction and momentum for parish life. We will be returning to these tables throughout the rest of this book.

I have a pen-and-pencil holder on my desk that has "The Essence of Leadership" inscribed on its side. Here are the words attributed to Douglas MacArthur: "A true leader has the confidence to stand alone, the courage to make tough decisions, and the compassion to listen to the needs of others. He or she does not set out to be a leader, but becomes one by the quality of his or her actions and the integrity of his or her intent. In the end, leaders are much like eagles, they don't flock; you find them one at a time."

As this exploration begins, let the reader note in that inscription the words *confidence, courage, decisions, listen, actions, integrity,* and *intent*. I plant them here as seeds; you will find them sprouting up throughout this book. Let me also warn, ever so gently, the pastor who prefers solo flights and displays lone-ranger tendencies that he can be aloof without realizing it, and unresponsive to the wisdom and will of those he is there to lead.

Leadership can more easily be described than defined. It is worth the effort, however, here at the outset, to attempt a definition.

Let me first take a moment to mention the often-expressed notion that "we are all leaders." To a certain and not unimportant extent, this is true. The expression provides a necessary corrective to the command-and-control, "somebody-has-to-be-in-charge" understanding of leadership. But if everyone is in charge, can we clearly identify a locus of leadership? Can we locate the decision point? Will we know when and where to move? In any given situation—whether it be a crisis or just a good time for change—if everyone is a leader, is leadership in fact there? It can be, but where?

In my view, the way out of this thicket lies in a distinction between taking charge and exerting influence. "Influencer" is an unfamiliar, perhaps misleading, and surely awkward term. "Leader" is so much more familiar; it is easier on the ear and smoother on the tongue. Let me suggest, therefore, that you think of the leader as an influencer who has been shaped by countless other influences and influencers. Together, leader and led constitute a rising tide of influence or a prevailing influential wind because of which change occurs, progress happens. Leaders do indeed influence others, but there is more to leadership than influence.

Think of the really successful, generally outstanding parish. One, several, or a relatively few persons are out there on the point, but all are responsible for the leadership that has taken place. This is the meaning I attach to the saying, "We are all leaders." We are; but I would want to add, "Some more than others." And in a Catholic parish, it is the pastor's job to bring those few together, to keep them talking to one another, and to support them with praise and encouragement. "Spray the place with praise" was the advice given by a veteran pastor to a new young pastor many years ago. Hard to improve on that!

"Followership" is the ultimate test of leadership. That seems fairly obvious. If you are going to lead, someone has to follow. Hence, my personal definition of leadership is "the art of inducing others to follow." A variant on that would be, "the art of inducing change," because change is really the name of the leadership game.

Leadership is, from any point of view and by any measure, an art, the art of inducing others to follow. Leaders have to maximize their power to persuade; without persuasion, leadership simply does not happen.

Leadership is, moreover, modeled behavior. The leader shows others the way and they can see the way because they observe it in the leader. To be a leader is to lead by example. Followers follow what they see in their leader. Any organization can be thought of as a big machine; all its moveable parts are people. The leadership challenge is to get those people moving! Persuasion releases the brake and ignites forward progress.

Leadership is not a science (although there are indeed theories of leadership), nor is it a craft (although leaders "make" things happen by "carving out" solutions, "hammering down" loose ends, and "fixing" broken policies). Just as politics is often called "the art of the possible," leadership is the art of getting things done willingly (if not always cheerfully) by the coordinated efforts of others. Why not think of the leader as an artist, if leadership is, in fact, an art? I think we should. And the image of an artist can serve as a helpful corrective to the king-of-the-hill, leader-as-hero image that many uncritically assume to be an accurate portrayal of real leadership.

Time now to move on to a reflection on parish leadership, but first I want to mention that Chapter 6 ("The Servant Leader") draws upon material that first appeared in print as Chapter 13 in my book

Next-Generation Leadership (University of Scranton Press, 2010), and that portions of Chapter 10 ("Change Is at the Heart of Leadership") come from that same book. Chapter 8 ("Facing Up to the Clergy Sex Abuse Scandal") is based on an article of mine that appeared under the title of "Structural Adjustments for a Church Working Its Way through Crisis," *Church* magazine (Winter 2004, pp.11–16).

CHAPTER One

Shared Spirituality for Parish Leadership

It is natural to think of spirituality when one thinks of parish life and a parish leadership team. And it is important to open this narrative with a reflection on spirituality by way of preamble to all administrative considerations.

According to theologian Doris Donnelly, spirituality is prayer elevated to a lifestyle. That's one compelling definition of the reality that in these stressful times is prompting countless persons in, out of, and around the church to stretch their souls toward God. Affairs are now "soul size," as playwright Christopher Fry phrased it in *A Sleep of Prisoners*, and "the enterprize is exploration into God."[1] If it is happening in the broader culture, it should certainly be happening at the top of any effective parish organization. Prayerful people should be in charge.

Shared spirituality is the foundation for effective parish leadership. This assumes that the leadership responsibility is shared. It is not command-and-control, top-down, Father-knows-best.

The cultural question "What is spirituality?" gives rise to another question: What are the roots of our current growing interest in spiritual issues in and out of religious circles?

More than sixty years ago in the U.S., *Time* magazine ran a cover story about an event that shook the world, an event that wounded many so profoundly that it has remained to trouble many of us, mind and soul, ever since. The incident, which was reported in the August 20, 1945, issue of the magazine, marked both an end and a beginning.

This report was published, as were all *Time* stories in those days, without attribution of authorship. I learned years later that a young (and then relatively unknown) Time staffer by the name of James Agee wrote the piece under a very tight deadline. The overarching headline was "Victory." The first subhead was "The Peace." The second subhead was "The Bomb."

Time was covering a big story that week, perhaps the biggest of the century. Agee, who later became famous as a writer, saw the "controlled splitting of the atom" that produced the bomb that was used to attack Hiroshima and Nagasaki, and thus bring to an end the greatest conflict in human history, as an event so enormous that in comparison "the war itself shrank to minor significance." To Agee's eye, "[H]umanity, already profoundly perplexed and disunified, was brought inescapably into a new age in which all thoughts and things were split—and far from controlled."[2]

Time's readers, still dizzy with the thrill of victory, could hardly have seen, as Agee did, the potential for both good and evil that the atomic bomb represented.

> The promise of good and evil bordered alike on the infinite—with this further, terrible split in the fact: that upon a people already so nearly drowned in materialism even in peacetime, the good uses of this power might easily bring disaster as prodigious as the evil.... When the bomb split open the universe...it also revealed the oldest, simplest, commonest, most neglected and most important of facts: that each man is eternally and above all else responsible for his own soul, and in the terrible words of the Psalmist, that no man may deliver his brother, nor make agreement unto God for him.[3]

Then Agee made a shattering observation that rings every bit as true today as it did that memorable August many years ago. Here are the words he wrote—words that were available to any reader of America's most popular newsmagazine in 1945 and that have gone largely unheeded in the decades since:

> Man's fate has forever been shaped between the hands of reason and spirit, now in collaboration, again in conflict. Now reason and spirit meet on final ground. If either or anything is to survive, they must find a way to create an indissoluble partnership.[4]

These powerful words were perceptive and prophetic. They appeared just before the so-called "baby boomers" were born. They explain the cause of the "split" that has been troubling humanity for well over half a century. We have not yet forged the "indissoluble partnership" between reason and spirit (reason, which produced the bomb; spirit, which must manage its control); we are even more adrift now than we were then on a sea of materialism. We may, however, be beginning to notice what Agee saw when the bomb split open the universe, namely, that each of us is responsible for his or her own soul.

Men and women in the world of work who are restless and wondering about the relevance of their Sunday faith to their Monday responsibilities are, I believe, being nudged now by the Spirit—the Holy Spirit—to begin an exploration into God. Their parishes should be helping them to do this.

"Spirituality" is not to be confused with the everyday sense of the word "spirit"—as in "school spirit," "pioneer spirit," the "spirit of capitalism," or the "spirited" response someone might make to some external stimulus. To be *spirited* in such contexts is to react to something completely human, something finite. That which is truly *spiritual* is immaterial and cannot be fully grasped by our limited human minds; it cannot be measured, counted, weighed, or touched. It is seen only in its effects.

3

Spirit in a faith-based spirituality rooted in the Christian tradition is identified with the Holy Spirit, the Third Person of the triune God, present and active in the human soul. As scripture puts it: "This is how we know that we remain in [God] and he in us, that he has given us of his Spirit" (1 Jn 4:13).

In his Letter to the Galatians, Paul addresses people who are converts from paganism. He instructs them in the exercise of their newfound freedom in the Holy Spirit and urges them to "live by the Spirit" in their normal secular surroundings. This is precisely what serious Christians at work in the world today are concerned about doing. This is also what should be preoccupying those at the leadership level in parishes today.

How can one know that he or she is "guided by the Spirit?" Take a look at The Pauline Criteria.

St. Paul offers in Galatians 5:22–23 what I call the Pauline Criteria for judging the consistency of one's own (or anyone else's) behavior with the presence of the Spirit in a human life. They constitute what Paul calls the "fruit of the Spirit." Note the singular fruit; these are not the gifts of the Holy Spirit; they are a set of Pauline principles. There are nine of them. Paul lists them in this order:

1. Love
2. Joy
3. Peace
4. Patience
5. Kindness
6. Generosity
7. Faithfulness
8. Gentleness
9. Self-Control

Examine what you do at home or in the workplace—particularly if that workplace happens to be a pastoral center—against these criteria. Judge another's oppositional or supportive behavior in that same workplace in the light of these norms. These are non-market values that can humanize every marketplace and workplace, not to mention the special place associated with parish work and worship.

Notice that Paul has not outlined unattainable goals. All nine of these Pauline characteristics are within your reach; they are attainable by normal people leading ordinary lives.

In contrast to these ingredients of a faith-based spirituality rooted in Christian revelation, Paul mentions the "works of the flesh," i.e., human activity only, activity not informed by God's indwelling Spirit. The works of the flesh are what we are left with when we reject the Spirit and set out blindly on our own. These rebel elements are "obvious," Paul notes, and he identifies them as follows: "immorality, impurity, licentiousness, idolatry, sorcery, hatreds, rivalry, jealousy, outbursts of fury, acts of selfishness, dissensions, factions, occasions of envy, drinking bouts, orgies, and the like" (Gal 5:19–21). At the end of this catalogue, Paul puts it bluntly: "I warn you, as I warned you before, that those who do such things will not inherit the kingdom of God" (Gal 5:21).

After examining Paul's second list, you might be forgiven for thinking to yourself, "Well, except for the orgies, that's actually a pretty fair description of the workplace as I know it." An exaggeration, of course, but all the more reason to focus closely on the first list of positive Pauline values.

If spirituality is to mean anything at all for you in the workplace, the Pauline Criteria signaling the presence of the Spirit must become the very infrastructure you carry with you into the world of work. And this is especially the case in the parish workplace. They should be guiding principles, pillars that support your working life. The Pauline Criteria can transform you, and with them you can transform the workplace. If you hope to change the world around you, first change yourself!

Sober reflection on the absence in your surroundings (and perhaps even in yourself) of these positive criteria can be unsettling. So can the realization of the occasional presence of what Paul listed as negatives. These experiences should be unsettling. Welcome the discomfort. It can serve an eviction notice on the complacency that can stifle the Spirit and the spirituality waiting to energize you from within your soul. Let's look now in detail at each of the nine Pauline values.

LOVE

The word means many things to many people. Popular culture debases love in song and story, forever confusing it with physical passion. Great literature and great lives through the centuries display the profound beauty of truly selfless love.

At bottom, love is service and sacrifice. It is the willingness to lay down one's life—literally or figuratively—for another. When you think about love, you should be thinking about your willingness to offer up your own true self for the benefit of another.

JOY

Joy is another profound reality that is not to be misunderstood. It is not to be confused with pleasure or hilarity. Those who replace the "pursuit of happiness" with the pursuit of *pleasure* will find lasting joy always eluding them. Joy is an inner assurance that your will is aligned with God's will, that you are favored, graced, and gifted beyond anything that you could merit on your own. Joy is balance, an abiding contentment.

PEACE

Often mistaken for whatever follows a truce, peace is actually tranquility. St. Thomas Aquinas described it as the "tranquility of right order." Those who "bury the hatchet" and retain their grudges are not at peace. Those who retain their emotional balance and agree to disagree, can live in harmony.

PATIENCE

This word literally means "suffering." The agent acts; the "patient" receives the action. How the person receives the action—especially the unwelcome action—is the test of patience. Tests of patience arise from countless sources: a dentist's drill; a honking horn; a fist pounding on the table; a spoken contradiction; an unmerited rebuke. The question is: How do you respond?

KINDNESS

Many have remarked that apparent kindnesses can, in fact, be acts of cruelty. This means that weakness or timidity can slip into virtue's clothing, and provide cover for an escape from responsibility or right action. Many a selfish or hypocritical act has been justified by a bad motive that is wrapped in counterfeit kindness.

Kindness does not depend on the perceptions of others. True kindness is respect for human dignity in *every* circumstance of life; it is both courtesy and personally courageous attentiveness displayed toward another person.

GENEROSITY

The opposite of all that is small, closed, petty, ungiving, and unforgiving, generosity points to largeness of soul. Generosity does not come naturally to human nature. But generosity can be learned by observation and acquired by practice. Whenever practiced, true generosity demonstrates the truth of the dictum that virtue is its own reward.

FAITHFULNESS

Dependability and reliability are the prerequisites of friendship. Keeping commitments— commonly thought of as "promises" and theologically understood as "covenants"—is the "stuff" of faith.

For the believer, faith is the habit of entrusting oneself to God. In the workplace, faithfulness is friendship, trust, and the security derived from commitments kept. These two varieties of "promises kept" may seem separate, but they actually reflect a single ongoing reality in the life of the believer.

GENTLENESS

Automobile executive Lee Iacocca, when at the height of his business career as chairman of the Chrysler Corporation, was referred to by a speaker at a black-tie dinner in New York City as a "gentle" man (aren't all who attend such functions "ladies and gentlemen"?). The flamboyant entrepreneur Donald Trump followed the speaker to present an award to Iacocca and ridiculed the suggestion that there was anything at all "gentle" about him.

Does being a "gentle" man (or woman) imply refinement? withdrawal? a retiring personality? What *does* it mean to be gentle? Gentleness is so often confused with timidity that we are caught in a cultural confusion over the very meaning of the word, and of the place of gentleness in the workplace.

In actuality, gentleness is strength. The gentle person is neither insecure nor arrogant; he or she is self-possessed, in quiet control of self and the surrounding situation.

SELF CONTROL

This test of personal integrity involves the practice of saying no to the self. A young mother once held up her infant son in the presence of the legendary American Civil War general Robert E. Lee and asked for his blessing on the child. Lee offered an apt but rare and unusual blessing: "Teach him he must deny himself," Lee said.

A person "out of control" in matters large or small is a diminished person. To have "lost it" in any circumstance of life, is to have abdicated that which makes one human; it is to have invited a curse and rejected a blessing.

WELCOMING THE SPIRIT—EVERY DAY

Anyone seriously concerned with the challenge of changing work-place negatives (especially in a parish workplace) into faith-based positives, or with welcoming the Spirit to dwell within his or her own soul, might well begin with Paul's nine-point checklist, making it an instrument of personal and private daily self-examination. These nine pillars can support an ongoing commitment to the development of a personal spirituality.

A practical spirituality for life and work can become a personal part of you if you simply follow these suggestions:

- Write these spiritual guidelines down as a nine-point check-list in score-card style.

- Reflect on them prayerfully for a few moments in the morning as you ask God's blessing on your day.

- Then, in the evening, again in a few moments of reflective prayer, review your checklist and mark your slippage or progress on each point as you give thanks to God for all the gifts that are yours at the close of another day.

Such a routine is quite simple: A morning and evening expression of gratitude accompanied by a checklist review. As simple as it is, however, this approach to spirituality—or any approach vaguely resembling it—is all too rare in modern life. What a difference it would make for any home or workplace if everyone who interacted there attended to Paul's checklist at the beginning and end of every day! And it goes without saying that this could be transformative for a parish workplace.

A PERSONAL CHECKLIST

Before your working day begins and at the end of the day before going to bed, compose yourself for a few moments of stocktaking in prayer. You may want to use the following as a starting point for developing your own routine, but avoid the rote repetition of empty words and phrases. Be sure to allow for your own formulation of questions and selection of points for emphasis.

- Recall that you are in God's presence, and thank God for the gift of life and any other gifts that come to mind.

- Ask for light to see yourself as God sees you, to see your day in the light of eternity.

Review your role in the day just unfolding, or just ending, against these norms:

Love
Morning: Am I prepared to share, serve, sacrifice for others today?
Evening: Did I open up toward others? Where did I hurt anyone or hold back?

Joy
Morning: Is my will aligned with God's? Do I cherish the graces, the gifts of God to me? Do I recognize the difference between pleasure and happiness? Am I in balance?
Evening: Where did I turn in on myself today? When and why did sadness touch me today? Did I lose balance?

Peace
Morning: What image of tranquility can I carry with me into this new day?

Evening: Why was I upset? What grudges am I carrying? Did I disturb the peace of others? Did I make anyone angry?

Patience

Morning: Am I prepared to suffer today, if God wills it or is willing to permit it?

Evening: When and why did I "lose it" today? Did I over-react? Did I lose my temper because I was about to lose face? Do I really believe that everything depends on me?

Kindness

Morning: Am I prepared to be considerate today? Will courtesy and civility accompany me through the day, and will attentiveness mark my relationship to others?

Evening: Did I contribute any rudeness, abrupt demands, or insults to the rubble of this day?

Generosity

Morning: What will I be today, a giver or a taker?

Evening: Was I petty, ungiving, or unforgiving in any way today? Did meanness enter the world today through me? Did I make anyone smile? Did I listen generously?

Faithfulness

Morning: If God is God, he cannot be anything but faith-ful to me today and always. I resolve to remain faithful to God today and, with God's help, to keep all my commitments in faith and friendship, in dependability and reliability.

Evening: Was anyone let down by me today? Did I lose any faith in God or in myself? Did I violate any trusts?

Gentleness

Morning: I am capable of being rude, rough, and domineering. I want to be gentle. I hope the source of all gentleness will work through me today.

Evening: Was I harsh toward anyone today? Did I hurt anyone in any way?

Self Control

Morning: I may have to say no to myself today; am I ready?

Evening: Did I leave any space for others today? Was I selfish or indulgent in ways that diminished the world's supply of human dignity?

Again, give thanks and, as needed, express not just regret but resolve to make amends.

Consider developing a daily sheet for monitoring your activity in each of the nine areas. Blank spaces on that sheet will allow you to monitor your own personal progress with regard to each of the Pauline values.

One item or another on the list of nine may call for special attention at a given stage in your life; you can highlight any category you like. You can also add other criteria that suit your purposes. Remember: The point of any exercise involving the Pauline Criteria is to heighten your awareness of God's presence in your life, and your responses to or rejections of God's promptings to you in the course of any day.

If these Pauline Criteria for the presence of the Spirit in a human life are internalized, if they become part of who you are regardless of what you do for a living, you will carry them with you to your place of employment and it will become so much the better place for your presence there. But this raises the question of why you are there in the first place, and that is a question of vocation. What is your calling? Everyone has one. What is yours?

As a youngster growing up in Philadelphia, I frequently heard the word "vocation" used in either of two ways: a "vocational school," like Dobbins, where students uninterested or unqualified for enrollment elsewhere on an "academic track" took carpentry, printing, or other "vocational" courses so that they could "get a job." Or the word referred to some form of religious ministry. In a religious context, Protestant ministers were "called" to serve a particular congregation; young Catholics were urged to consider a "vocation" to priesthood or religious life as something special that was given by God; the "call" was not to be taken lightly. If accepted, a vocation was, in the pious imagination, carried around much like a piece of air-travel luggage that could be "lost" at almost any point on the journey. Anyone who refused or lost this "higher calling" was thought to be running no small degree of personal, spiritual risk.

This misleading vocabulary has fallen out of fashion now. Young people are encouraged to think not in terms of having or losing a vocation, but of *being* a vocation. You *are* a vocation, is the theologically correct perspective to take on this question. You are responding to a call from the God who formed you in your mother's womb, called you then, and never stops calling. It is not as if God placed a call to you, left a message on your answering machine, and then hung up. No, you are being called, person-to-person, at every moment of your life. Do not, however, expect to hear a voice. You can hear this call in the circumstances of your life, in your temperament and talents, in your physical and intellectual capacities, in your aspirations and desires. All of these are gifts to you from God. Faith instructs you to use them according to God's will for your salvation, for his glory, and for the service of your fellow human beings. That is what you are "called" by God to be and to do. And because God calls you to do it, the work—whatever it is—has dignity. Martin Luther King once said, "If a man is called to be a streetsweeper, he should sweep streets even as Michelangelo painted, or Beethoven composed music, or Shakespeare wrote poetry. He should sweep streets so well that all the hosts of heaven and earth will pause to say, here lived a great streetsweeper who did his job well."[5]

There is, I want to emphasize, a genuine vocation to what anyone in any organization is doing, to where you find yourself, top or bottom, in the world of work. You are not a random fluctuation in some complex system of occupational distribution. You are a person who is known and cherished by a creator-God who has something special for you in mind. Even if prayer was the furthest thing from your mind when you prepared yourself for a particular way of life—taking this job or that, selecting one profession over another, living here or there—God was not disinterested or disengaged from the process. God's providence was there at least permitting and perhaps promoting the outcome of your unreflective choices. Regardless of the presence or absence of prayerful reflection on your part as you moved through life to where you are at this present moment (and, remember, you are a vocation), you can decide now to begin listening more attentively to the God who calls; you can attempt to read more carefully the will of God in the circumstances where you find yourself right now.

I've always liked this reflection-prayer of John Henry Cardinal Newman. It is one of the "ponderables" that belongs in any workplace spirituality. It is an assertion of purpose and vocation even when you are tempted to believe that your compass is gone and your life is devoid of meaning.

> God has created me to do Him some definite service; He has committed some work to me which He has not committed to another. I have my mission—I may never know it in this life, but I shall be told it in the next....
>
> I am a link in a chain, a bond of connection between persons. He has not created me for naught. I shall do good; I shall do His work; I shall be an angel of peace, a

preacher of truth in my own place, while not intending it, if I do but keep His commandments and serve in His calling.

Therefore, I will trust Him. Whatever, wherever, I am, I can never be thrown away. If I am in sickness, my sickness may serve him; in perplexity, my perplexity may serve Him; if I am in sorrow, my sorrow may serve Him....He does nothing in vain.... He knows what He is about. He may take away my friends, He may throw me among strangers, He may make me feel desolate, make my spirits sink, hide the future from me—still He knows what He is about.[6]

So, here you are at this moment with these thoughts offered to assist you in connecting your religious faith to your workplace life. This chapter is intended especially for those whose workplace will be a parish setting. The point of this integration is to enable you to deal productively not only with the wounds and reversals that are part of any life anywhere, but with the challenges that are yours in the workplace to make God present in this world, to make life better for others, to do something with your life that aligns your life with God's will for you. The integration of religious faith and workplace responsibilities will bring balance to your life. And if you are called to a leadership position there, you can create a workplace culture within which those you direct can themselves lead a balanced life.

Spirit-driven leaders will facilitate this process in a quiet, almost imperceptible way. The result will be

Spirit-driven followers or associates whose presence in a workplace will witness to a workplace transformed.

For this to happen, much will depend on your willingness to let these spiritual truths sink into your soul as moisture seeps into the earth.

It will not happen right away or all at once. Let these lines from Robert Frost's poem *Snow* set the pace for the process of your personal assimilation of the wisdom principles that will keep you on track in stressful times:

> Our very life depends on everything's
> Recurring till we answer from within.
> The thousandth time may prove the charm.[7]

Answers "from within" are wisdom principles; they rise from the depths of a personal faith-based spirituality. They can push themselves up through emotion, confusion, anger, pride—through any of the negatives that will appear from time to time on your screen during the recommended review sketched out for you above. It won't happen automatically or right away. It might take awhile—"the thousandth time may prove the charm." But when it happens you have a spirituality up and running, ready to keep you on track and happy in your transit through life.

And, as you may have noticed, if this catches on in you and those around you at work, you have the makings of a truly collaborative workplace. Who can say where that will lead? A Spirit-driven leader might have an answer to that question. Moreover a Spirit-driven leader is a living answer to the skeptic or honest inquirer who wonders aloud about the relevance of all this to the real world. Is the spirituality outlined here viable in the push-and-shove, give-and-take, win-and-lose workplace world? As Jesus said in another context, "Come, and you will see" (Jn 1:39). I answer that question by saying: just take a look at any Spirit-driven leader at work in the world—and there are lots of them—and you will see for yourself. Then go and do likewise!

For those who insist that they have to be tough in order to lead, to "give as good as they get" in those "in-your-face," real-world exchanges, I say: think about that for a moment. Do you really want to stand at the door before going into what will surely be a difficult negotiating session or demanding meeting, and say, "Okay, Holy Spirit, you have to wait outside. I've got work to do. I'm leaving love, joy, peace, patience and all that other stuff out here so that I can go in there and get something done!"? No; of course not.

Instead, wrap yourself in an imaginary coat of mail made up of those nine strands that I've been calling the Pauline Criteria. If they're not there, neither is the Holy Spirit. You decide.

As I suggested earlier, it is the responsibility of the pastor, first to assimilate these principles in himself and then to foster their growth in every member of the pastoral service team. I don't promise that it will be easy. I do promise that it will be transformative. Try bringing them to the table for meetings of the parish staff and notice the difference that follows.

CHAPTER Two

Applying the Tradition of Catholic Social Teaching to Parish Leadership

The integration of Catholic social teaching into the fabric of parish life has the potential of transforming parish life. But it won't happen unless the principles are first internalized by those entrusted with the leadership of parish life. If it seems strange to devote a lengthy chapter on the principles of Catholic social teaching to a book on parish leadership, I ask the reader to bear with me. The absence of both the letter and spirit of Catholic social teaching from contemporary parish life explains the failure of many parishes to connect with the people and to evangelize effectively, indeed the failure of many parishes to be effective at all.

The introduction of Catholic social teaching might well appear to be the application of a second layer of infrastructure to this overall consideration of parish leadership. And that would not be wide of the mark. Pope Francis has gone to great pains to remind Catholics worldwide that the social teaching of their church is an essential part of Catholic life. It belongs in the parish, but it will not find a place there unless it first finds its place in the minds and hearts of those called to leadership in a given Catholic parish. Subsequent chapters will discuss preaching and sacramental life as well as organizational structure in parishes; attention must first be paid to the Catholic treasury of social teaching.

I'll be concerned in this chapter with explaining the following ten principles of Catholic social thought:

- The Principle of Human Dignity

- The Principle of Respect for Human Life

- The Principle of Solidarity

- The Principle of Preferential Protection for the Poor and Vulnerable

- The Principle of Participation

- The Principle of Human Equality (Justice)

- The Principle of Stewardship

- The Principle of Association

- The Principle of Subsidiarity

- The Principle of the Common Good

This list of ten represents an effort on my part to condense or digest the essentials of the tradition of Catholic social teaching. They are a summary of a body of doctrine that is to be communicated, discussed, and, one would hope, assimilated in Catholic education, but my immediate concern is with the assimilation of these principles in parish life. They should shape the parish culture and thus influence the choices made by all who interact there.

A culture, as Bernard Lonergan would define it, is a set of shared meanings, principles, and values. Values define cultures. Where values are widely shared and the sharing bonds together with common ties those who hold the same values, you have an identifiable culture. There are as many different cultures as there are distinct sets of shared meanings, principles, and values. This is not to say that everyone in a given culture is the same. No; you have diversity of age, wealth, class, intelligence, education, and responsibility in a given culture where diverse people are unified by a shared belief system, a set of agreed-upon principles, a collection of common values. They literally have a lot in common and thus differ from people in other settings who hold a lot of other things in common. You notice it in law firms, hospitals, colleges, corporations—wherever people comment on the special "culture" that characterizes the place. You should be able to notice it in a parish—something valued, something shared, something special that sets the place apart. These should shape a parish culture, but they are largely unknown in the typical parish. It is important, therefore, to consider them now—up front—before considering the more familiar aspects of parish life.

THE PRINCIPLE OF HUMAN DIGNITY

The principle of human dignity is the first on my list of ten principles of Catholic Social Teaching. As I mentioned earlier, principles, once internalized, lead to something. They prompt activity, impel motion, direct choices.

In 1998, the National Conference of Catholic Bishops (now the United States Conference of Catholic Bishops) issued *Sharing Catholic Social Teaching: Challenges and Directions—Reflections of the U.S. Catholic Bishops*, a document intended to call the attention of all U.S. Catholics to the existence of Catholic social principles—a body of doctrine with which, the bishops said, "far too many Catholics are not familiar." In fact, they added, "many Catholics do not adequately understand that the social teaching of the Church is an essential part of Catholic faith." These are strong words that should be taken seriously.

A companion document, "Summary Report of the Task Force on Catholic Social Teaching and Catholic Education," is included in the same booklet that contains the bishops' reflections on this "serious challenge for all Catholics."

The task force, of which I was a member, was convened in 1995 by the late Archbishop John R. Roach, then retired archbishop of St. Paul-Minneapolis. Often during our periodic meetings over the course of two years, it occurred to me that one (admittedly only one) reason why the body of Catholic social teaching is underappreciated, under-communicated and not sufficiently understood is that the principles on which the doctrine is based are not clearly articulated and conveniently condensed. They are not "packaged" for catechetical purposes like the Ten Commandments and the Seven Sacraments. While many Catholics can come up with the eight Beatitudes and some would be willing to take a stab at listing the four cardinal virtues, few, if any, have a ready reply to the catechetical question the bishops wanted to raise: What are those Catholic social principles that are to be accepted as an essential part of the faith? The next question, of course, looks to how they can best be personally appropriated—internalized—so that they can lead to action.

On the tenth anniversary of their 1986 pastoral letter "Economic Justice for All," the bishops issued a summary of their teaching on the applicability of Catholic social principles to the economy. We on the task force had that summary in mind as we considered the broader issue of the applicability of Catholic social thought to a range of issues that go beyond the economic to include family, religious issues, social, political, technological, recreational and cultural considerations. It would be a mistake, of course, to confine Catholic social teaching to the economic sphere. Its applicability is far wider.

How many Catholic social principles are there? Combing through the documents mentioned above, I have come up with ten. There is nothing at all official about my count. Some future *Catechism of the Catholic Church* may list more or fewer than these ten, if compilers of that future teaching aid find that Catholic social teaching is suitable for framing in such a fashion. I offer my list of ten here for three reasons: (1) Some reasonably complete list is needed if the ignorance cited by the bishops is going to be addressed; (2) any list can serve to invite the hand of both editors and teachers to smooth out the sentences for clarity and ease of memorization; and (3) any widely circulated list will stimulate further thought on the part of scholars and activists as to what belongs in a set of principles that can serve as a table of contents for the larger body of Catholic social teaching. So,

I offer here ten principles of Catholic social thought and will begin with the Principle of Human Dignity in my effort to integrate all ten into a better understanding of parish leadership.

PRINCIPLE OF HUMAN DIGNITY

"Every human being is created in the image of God and redeemed by Jesus Christ, and therefore is invaluable and worthy of respect as a member of the human family"[8]. Those words are taken from the 1998 document issued by the Catholic bishops of the United States that I alluded to above. This is the bedrock principle of Catholic social teaching. Every person—regardless of race, sex, age, national origin, religion, sexual orientation, employment or economic status, health, intelligence, achievement or any other differentiating characteristic—is worthy of respect. It is not what you do or what you have that gives you a claim on respect; it is simply *being* human that establishes your dignity. Given that dignity, the human person is, in the Catholic view, never a means, always an end.

As I said, this is the bedrock principle of Catholic social teaching and indeed of all personal and social ethics. Just take a moment to think about the state of human dignity in today's world, let alone in the territorial limits of your own parish—think of world hunger, for example, think of the unemployed, the human beings who are mentally or physically ill, the illiterate, the homeless. Think of the condition of human dignity in your own country, town or city. Do you ever think of assaults on human dignity or neglect of those in need as sinful? I like the following definition of sin that I've lifted from the Japanese writer Shushaku Endo's novel *Silence*. Endo was a 20th century Japanese Catholic writer of great renown. In *Silence*, his protagonist is a Jesuit missionary to Japan. Endo has Fr. Sebastio Rodrigues sitting alone in a prison cell listening to guards outside—laughing and talking, having no regard for him. Indeed they reminded him of the guards who cast lots for the garments of Jesus before he was taken off to die. In any case, here are the words from the novel:

> "These guards, too, were men; they were indifferent
> to the fate of others. This was the feeling that their
> laughing and talking stirred up in his heart [the impris-
> oned priest]. Sin, he reflected, is not what it is usually
> thought to be; it is not to steal and tell lies. Sin is for
> one man to walk brutally over the life of another and
> to be quite oblivious of the wounds he has left behind."[9]

Human dignity is taking a beating in contemporary society. We have to begin noticing. We have to wonder why. We have to notice that human beings are walking over the lives of other human beings, and we have to wonder to what extent we, by our direct actions or inaction, or our indirect participation or complicity with the actions of others, are part of the problem. Just think of how we tolerate, even enjoy, violence in entertainment. We take violence so much for granted without giving any thought at all to the damage it does to the human dignity of those who receive it as well as those who inflict it.

Workers at all levels are being treated as if they were disposable parts. In many cases, bottom lines and balance sheets get more attention than human beings (too often regarded as human doings) who lose their jobs to "reengineered" processes or to "reinvention" in the workplace. We simply cannot afford to forget the point made so directly by Pope Pius XI in 1931 in his great encyclical On Reconstructing the Social Order (*Quadragesimo anno*). He minced no words: "Dead matter leaves the factory ennobled and transformed, where men are corrupted and degraded."[10] The point is that human beings are diminished in the very process of enhancing dead matter and bringing it to market.

Pornography and prostitution are widespread in contemporary society. They represent massive assaults on human dignity, as do hunger, homelessness, torture, and neglect. The list is long.

It is interesting to note that the expression *human dignity* found its way into the mainstream of official social teaching of the Church in the form of the title of the famous Declaration on Religious Liberty in the Second Vatican Council. That document begins with the Latin words "Dignitatis humanae" (Of Human Dignity). The right to religious freedom is based on the dignity of the human person. The document speaks of human dignity in setting the tone for what it has to say about religious freedom; it makes the central point that respect for religious freedom rises out of a consciousness of human dignity on the part of the Church. In function of his or her inviolable human dignity, every person has a right to "immunity from external coercion in matters religious."[11]

The other nine principles on my list of ten constitute what I like to think of as a social justice imperative; they represent a compendium of Catholic social thought, and they need to find their proper place in the consciousness of every committed Catholic. This is an enormous contemporary challenge confronting every parish leader.

THE PRINCIPLE OF HUMAN LIFE

The next principle to be discussed in this set of ten principles of Catholic Social Teaching is the Principle of Respect for Human Life. We looked at human dignity; now the focus is on human life. Let me begin by outlining the reasons that underlie my own pro-life convictions. A short sentence in the Nov. 24, 2008, Associated Press report on issues in the then-upcoming policy debate over whether or not the ban on federal funding for embryonic stem cell research should be lifted accurately portrays the argument against the use of embryonic stem cells by saying that "life begins at conception—that once fertilization occurred in the lab, so did a human being."[12] Hence no embryo should be destroyed in order to facilitate stem cell research. I subscribe to that argument, and I admire the verbal precision: "that once fertilization occurred…so did a human being."

The reference in the news story was, of course, to in vitro fertilization. But whether in the womb or in the laboratory, when fertilization occurs, there is life. This is undeniable. A *being* exists that did not exist before. Because it is human life—on its way to becoming more fully human—it is, the argument goes, a human being. To assert that it is not human because it is not yet fully human is to deny the reality that a continuum of existence has begun. This is not to say that the embryo is a human person; it may well be, but that is not the claim. The claim is simply that a *being* exists that is on its way to becoming fully human. To terminate, for purposes of research, what would otherwise be an inevitable biological development to full human personhood is morally wrong. That conclusion can be drawn from human reason without the guidance of divine revelation or the rulings of organized religion. Reason sees in the fertilized egg an incipient human person and concludes that this is a life worthy of respect and protection. Those who disagree and see no human life in this living being at the moment of conception are, in my view, not to be dismissed as having no respect at all for human life and dignity. They are, however, to be confronted on the issues of (1) when human life begins, (2) why any human life should not be regarded as a human being (if something exists, how can it not be?), and (3) why a developing human being has no claim on the possession of actual or potential personhood.

To engage in a verbally imprecise policy debate about embryonic vs. adult stem cell research would be to walk mindlessly past the possibility of widespread violation of human life, human rights, and human dignity. I would compare this to firing a rifle shot through a closed door when there is a possibility that a person is there on the other side.

We, as a nation, are not very good at engaging in verbally precise, reasoned argument on the life issues. The chances of that happening will improve, I think, if we show more respect for one another and permit ourselves to engage in respectful moral argument. This is a challenge to parish leadership—to get these conversations going. Beyond the parish, new forums may have to be found to facilitate this exchange. Whether the forum is a two-way conversation, a legislative debate, a group discussion, or a university seminar, the human hearts and human minds that shape the arguments and debate them will, I would hope, recognize and agree that they share one thing in common. They all possess a human life that began at the moment of conception. That is true for me; it is also true for anyone reading this book.

As I said, I think we need reasoned argument on abortion, not emotionally charged, accusatory and condemnatory rhetoric. It is no secret that wide-ranging debate has been going on in the political arena in the United States for many years on the abortion issue. It is not my intention to enter into that now. I do want, however, to suggest that the pro-life side of the debate should elaborate *moral* arguments (as opposed to arguments from authority, or arguments based on emotion, fear, or threat) for their position. I would also invite the so-called "pro choice" side of this debate to think about articulating a moral argument for any position on choice. All of us should be able to say we are "pro" any possible right and moral choice. The challenge, of course, lies in making the moral argument. And that challenge still confronts us.

Some conscientious persons may not equate human personhood with human life at its earliest stage of existence, but there is no denying that "it" is alive and will, if permitted to continue living, become a fully human person. Conversations and debates along these lines within either major political party will bring opposing positions up to the higher and common ground of respect for human life. This would, I believe, strengthen either party's convictions about improving things for the poor; avoiding unnecessary war; eliminating capital punishment; saving Social Security; advancing medical research; containing medical costs while extending medical coverage; improving the quality, efficiency, and effectiveness of education; defending the right of workers to organize and bargain collectively; protecting the human and civil rights of all minorities; assuring justice in law enforcement, taxation, and employment. In a certain sense, all of these are "life" issues.

On December 6, 1983, Cardinal Joseph Bernardin of Chicago gave a lecture at Fordham University in which he first articulated what he called a "consistent ethic of life."[13] He elaborated on this theme in countless talks and papers until his death in 1996. He insisted on extending discussion of the life issues beyond abortion to include capital punishment, assisted suicide, and euthanasia. And he employed a "seamless garment"[14] metaphor to encourage Catholics, in defending the sacredness of human life, to avoid the single-issue trap of a preoccupation with abortion. The Catholic eye should see the threats to human life embodied in all issues like those I've listed above; all aspects of healthcare, for example, represent an opportunity for pro-life support. And all these issues build on the principle of human dignity as well as the principle of respect for human life. But no progress will be made if the discussion takes place in a vacant vocabulary outside the range of reasoned argument. Nor will it help if each side simply aims pre-recorded messages at the other. It is time now to listen and talk to one another with respect.

In a speech at the University of Notre Dame in 1995, then Pennsylvania Governor Robert P. Casey said abortion is "like a bone in our throat. We can't swallow it. We cannot assimilate it. We cannot become comfortable with it, because it's fundamentally contrary to what we believe as Americans.... Every poll shows a vast and growing unease with the abortion license and the industry that serves it. I believe a pro-life consensus already exists in America. And it grows every time someone looks in a sonogram."

Reason, not religion, brought him to this conclusion. Reasoned argument will lead to conclusions that can be commended to all because of their consistency with the human nature shared by all, not necessarily because of their conformity with the tenets of a religion to which not all subscribe.

Whether the pro-life consensus Casey saw still is, or ever was, there, Democrats are going to have to look for an answer to this question within their own tradition of concern for the poor and vulnerable. If a consensus is there, they can find it and build on it. If not, they might think about developing one for the good of the nation, not just the good of the party. As the Jesuit theologian John Courtney Murray used to say, quoting the Dominican philosopher Thomas Gilby, civilizations are formed by citizens "locked together in argument."[15]

To brush all this aside as idealistic and impractical would be to miss the truth that there is, on occasion, nothing so practical as the right ideal. An ideal capable of bringing some unity within both Democratic and Republican ranks is the principle of respect for human dignity. Applied evenly across the board, this principle can strengthen either political party and help it make its own unique contribution to building a better nation through the give and take of politics.

THE PRINCIPLE OF SOLIDARITY

Catholic social teaching insists that we are our brothers' and sisters' keepers and therefore adds the principle of solidarity to its body of social doctrine. This principle has global dimensions in an interdependent world. It functions as a moral category that leads to choices that will promote and protect the common good. It translates the familiar "love-your-neighbor" commandment to *global* dimensions in the interdependent world that we all inhabit. We are indeed our brothers' and sisters' keepers. We are one large and growing family. Parish leadership fails its followership if it loses sight of the truly big picture.

The 1994 North American Free Trade Agreement (NAFTA) makes it impossible for U.S. business decision-makers to avoid facing up to the fact that free trade is an important vehicle that can carry our poor brothers and sisters in other parts of the world toward economic betterment. It will not be without cost to some beneficiaries of many decades of past economic development in the advanced countries including our own, but that is not a good reason to oppose free trade. If globalization means anything, it means globalization of markets with its promise, in the long run, of global economic justice and improvement for all. In this context, the "trade not aid" argument can, within proper limits, make a lot of sense.

This is a very complicated matter and arguments can be made that in certain cases free trade can hurt the poor nations. It is not my intention to get into complicated economic analysis here, or arguments pro or con on free trade. Nor do parish leaders have to get into all this. I do want, however, to try to unpack the notion of solidarity, a social category that holds an important place in the tradition of Catholic social thought and teaching and should be part of the mindset of every practicing Catholic.

The word "solidarity" was used by Pope Paul VI in his 1967 encyclical letter on the Development of Peoples (*Populorum progressio*). He wrote: "There can be no progress toward complete development of man without the simultaneous development of all humanity in the spirit of solidarity."[16]

Pope John Paul II picked up on that notion and translated "solidarity" into a moral category and gave it a prominent place in the tradition of Catholic social thought. He was a native of Poland. Karol Wojtyla was the Cardinal Archbishop of Krakow before being elected pope in 1978.

Another name worthy of recall is that of the Polish labor leader Lech Walesa. He was associated with the Polish trade union *Solidarność*—Solidarity—and as a young man worked as an electrician in Gdańsk shipyard. A strike in Gdańsk in 1980 led to the formation of the National Committee for Solidarity, and Walesa was elected chairman. It was the first independent labor union in a country belonging to the Soviet bloc. The union was suppressed by the Polish government but reemerged in 1989 and, with strong support from the Polish Pope—moral and spiritual support—Walesa was instrumental in the overthrow of Communism in the Soviet Union.

I can remember seeing in the 1980s the name SOLIDARITY in Polish lettering on a long banner that ran from the roof of the AFL-CIO Building on 16th Street in Washington, DC, down to the sidewalk. Lane Kirkland was then president of the AFL-CIO; he threw the support of the American labor movement behind the Polish organizing effort. Kirkland was a graduate of Georgetown's School of Foreign

Service. He was an internationally minded man. Some of his union members here at home thought he was too internationally minded, devoting more attention to the Solidarity movement in Poland than to efforts to grow the labor movement here at home. I don't want to get into that except to say that when Kirkland decided to retire and not run for re-election, the candidate he endorsed was not elected to the presidency of the AFL-CIO; they wanted someone whom they thought would focus on organizing here at home. I attended a memorial service for Lane Kirkland at Georgetown after his death in 1999, and I was impressed by the fact that Lech Walesa was there.

Walesa became Poland's first popularly elected president in 1990, having won the Nobel Peace Prize in 1983 for his stand against Communism. Solidarity became a familiar term here in the U.S.

Pope John Paul II laced it through various writings and did his best to bring it to the forefront of consciousness among Catholics as a moral category. Not only are we bound by a shared human nature with other humans around the world, we are bound to assist them — bound by a moral obligation because we are by nature in solidarity with them — to do what we can to advance human development in the backward areas of the world. Solidarity requires it of us.

John Paul II wanted solidarity to become what Robert Bellah would call a "habit of the heart," an internal driving principle directing the will toward the common good. For this pope, solidarity was not simply a principle; it was a virtue. It should affect your outlook and influence your choices.

As I will point out below in the discussing the preferential protection of the poor, the point is not to feel guilty. You may not know many poor people. You may not know anyone in Africa or Asia where millions of people are poor, malnourished, disease-ridden, dying. You may not know any of them, but you should be aware of their existence and mindful of the fact that you not only can but should help. How you help is up to you. But you cannot *not* help. Why? Because you share a human nature with the poor. Your human nature should put you in solidarity with them. And the principle of solidarity is a moral principle that conveys a moral obligation. You cannot shake it off. And if you ignore it, you do so at your moral peril.

Read *Laborem Excercens*, Pope John Paul II's encyclical about work, about human labor. And read another of his great social encyclicals, *Solicitudo Rei Socialis*, his 1987 letter "On Social Concern," and you'll meet the notion of solidarity throughout.

When the president of the United States sends his budget up to Congress each year, a debate begins over what might be cut and what can't be touched. Don't even think about cutting Social Security, protect Medicare by all means—the arguments are familiar. In the context of those arguments, it is always pointed out that the one area of the budget that is most vulnerable to cuts is foreign aid—food aid, financial assistance to developing countries, and the like. If solidarity is a moral category, and if Catholic Christians have a sense of solidarity with the poor in the developing world, why do not Catholic Christians speak up louder and more clearly in support of foreign assistance? They all live in parishes. Why has parish leadership failed to get them engaged?

Solidarity gives a horizontal dimension to our commitment to the common good, making it worldwide. Just as you might say that subsidiarity (to be considered later) gives a vertical dimension to our understanding of the common good, in the sense that decision-making can move up or down the line of authority in different circumstances in order to best serve the interests of the common good. So think flat—not flat world—but worldwide flat to the interests of our brothers and sisters all over the world when we are faced with keeping or cutting foreign aid. This, as any pastor who has attempted it will tell you, is not an easy sell.

Another term in the vocabulary of Catholic social thought, not unrelated to solidarity, is socialization. This one is often misunderstood, sometimes intentionally confused with socialism by those who are hostile to the principles of Catholic social thought; in any case, I think the notion of "socialization" is worthy of a brief mention here.

"Socialization" means simply an increase in social relationships and social responsibility. In his encyclical *Mater et Magistra*, Pope John XXIII called this "one of the principal characteristics of our time."[17] This, he says, involves "a daily, more complex interdependence of citizens, introducing into their lives and activities many and varied forms of association, recognized for the most part in private and even in public law."[18] The significance of John XXIII's recognition and support of socialization is that it marked the beginning of an effort to break the long alliance between Roman Catholicism and socially conservative forces. For example, the Catholic defense of the right to private property was used against the poor—i.e., used to maintain the status quo and oppose the union movement. Even today, opponents of health care reform call it socialism (which it surely is not) and try to impede or reverse efforts to extend healthcare insurance coverage to low-income people.

The connection to solidarity is obvious. As socialization spreads—i.e., as our social relationships widen beyond family, friends, and nation and become truly international—in other words, as our consciousness of connection deepens—so does our sense of solidarity and our social concern.

Our Catholic appreciation of socialization is an antidote to individualism. It also encourages us who are relatively well off in material terms to be genuinely concerned and caring for those who are not. Solidarity can link the rich with the poor if the rich, by God's grace, want it to be that way. Every Catholic is invited by the Church to face up to the question: Whose side are you on? All Catholics are invited to get off the beaten path. Drive through the cities, not around them. See the poverty, the unemployment, the addictions, the illnesses, the misfortunes— and try to feel for those less fortunate. This is what a sense of solidarity can do for you.

A PREFERENCE FOR THE POOR AND VULNERABLE

Next we turn to what is called the preferential love for the poor. I like to call it the Principle of Preferential Protection for the Poor and Vulnerable. And I do that for a purpose that I'll explain as I go along.

The tradition of Catholic social thought keeps alive the story of the last judgment (Mt 25:31-46) and emphasizes the importance of putting the needs of the poor and vulnerable first. Recall Matthew 25:

> "When the Son of Man comes in his glory, and all the angels with him, he will sit upon his glorious throne, and all the nations will be assembled before him. And he will separate them one from another, as a shepherd separates the sheep from the goats. He will place the sheep on his right and the goats on his left." (Mt 25:31–33)

And the gospel account goes on to explain that those on the right will hear their Lord say:

> "Come, you who are blessed by my Father. Inherit the kingdom prepared for you from the foundation of the world. For I was hungry and you gave me food, I was thirsty and you gave me drink, a stranger and you welcomed me, naked and you clothed me, ill and you cared for me, in prison and you visited me." (Mt 25:34–36)

And you will recall that the gospel story has those who hear these words say in reply:

> "Lord, when did we see you hungry and feed you, or thirsty and give you drink? When did we see you a stranger and welcome you, or naked and clothe you? When did we see you ill or in prison, and visit you?" And the king will say to them in reply, "Amen, I say to

you, whatever you did for one of these least brothers [or sisters] of mine, you did for me." (Mt 25:37–40)

And, of course, if you did not do it for the needy ones, the poor and vulnerable, you did not do it for him. There's a lesson there waiting to bother you whenever you refuse a beggar, ignore the ill, or forget the prisoner. Jesus intended it that way. He wanted to bother us. He wanted to stir up within us something resembling a social conscience.

Our Church teaches a preferential love for the poor because the common good—the good of society as a whole—requires it. The opposite of rich and powerful is poor and powerless. If the good of all, the common good, is to prevail, preferential protection must move toward those affected adversely by the absence of power and the presence of privation. Otherwise the balance needed to keep society in one piece will be broken to the detriment of the whole.

Any parent knows what preferential love means. The vulnerable three-year-old child gets preference over his or her more self-sufficient older sibling under certain circumstances. Let the toddler run out into the path of an oncoming automobile, and you'll see the older child left to fend for him- or herself on the sidewalk as the parent of both rushes out to extend preferential protection to the vulnerable child. So the modern Church is asking for nothing unusual, unfamiliar, or extraordinary when it calls for preferential love of the poor and vulnerable.

For those who find this truth hard, and many middle- and upper-class American Catholics do, the words of Pope John Paul II might be reassuring: "Love for the poor must be preferential, but not exclusive."[19] We can certainly conclude from this that those who happen not to be poor have no reason to conclude that they are not the constant object of God's unfailing love, but talk about "preferential love" often moves American middle class parishioners toward that false conclusion.

The Parable of the Rich man and Lazarus (Luke 16:19-31) is one of the texts most often cited in modern Catholic social teaching. The story of Dives and Lazarus, the rich man and the poor man, is a story of comfortable complacency on the side of Dives, the rich man, and the absence in him of a sense of justice, an absence of compassion and love. In their place we see purple garments, fine linen, and sumptuous dining in self-enclosed insensitivity.

Recall the words of Jesus, recorded at the beginning of the Gospel of Mark: "This is the time of fulfillment. The kingdom of God is at hand. Repent, and believe in the gospel" (Mark 1:15). Why has the kingdom been at hand now for over 2000 years but not yet grasped? Why is the fulfillment of love, justice, and peace not yet in our midst? Because we have refused to "repent," to change our hearts, to accept the attitudinal turnaround that is required of anyone who hears and really believes the gospel.

Millions have not yet heard the gospel in any meaningful way. Millions who have heard and accepted the Gospel have not yet let it turn them around in a true north direction toward love, justice, and peace.

As the story of Dives and Lazarus tells us, the poor man died and "was carried away by angels to the bosom of Abraham." And the rich man died, too, and wound up in the "netherworld, where he was in torment." His plea for pity and a drop of water was denied. It was too late. The book was closed. He was told that "between us and you a great chasm is established" and he couldn't cross it. So, the rich man pleaded that Lazarus be sent to warn the rich man's five surviving brothers "lest they too come to this place of torment." This drew another turndown from Abraham, who added that, if the living choose not to heed the teachings of Moses and the prophets, "neither will they be persuaded if someone should rise from the dead." (see Lk 16:19-31)

For us it is different. Someone did indeed rise from the dead. Jesus Christ, our Savior, faced death for our sake, passed through it for our salvation, made it possible for us to receive the gift of faith, and left behind for our consideration a gospel of justice and peace. What do you make of that gospel when you stop to think about it? Indeed, what do you make of the story of the rich man and the poor man, in the light of the violence and brokenness of the world in which we live?

We know that knowledge always comes before love and that most of us have little or no knowledge of the other nations, cultures, and religions that are in the headlines in the wake of the terrorist attacks. We have much to learn—about Islam, about Iraq, about Iran, about Afghanistan, and about people, religions, and cultures that differ from us.

The fact that we are surrounded by frightening events is no indication at all that we will be overcome by events. We live under the banner of the Cross. We have an interpretative framework within which to process the confusion, terror, and sorrow that have touched us quite literally where we live, as, for example, on September 11, 2001. We also have the Gospel calling us to love, justice, and peace, urging us to lower the human barriers that we permit to stand between us and the realization of justice, love, and peace in our lives, in our time. That kingdom is coming. We've got work to do. We've got to remove from ourselves and our human communities the roadblocks that our complacency permits to stand in the way of the coming reign of God.

So, ponder in prayer the reality of division and violence and injustice in your world and in your community today. Insert yourself into the scene that Luke's Gospel gives you so dramatically in the story of Dives and Lazarus. Insert yourself between the rich man and the poor man and give some prayerful thought as to what you might be called upon by God to do now to close the gap—what you can do with your charitable contributions, with your volunteer service, with the application of intellect in research, with the decisions you make with respect to choice of profession or occupation when your formal education ends. Parish leadership should be fostering this kind of pondering.

In citing this Scripture story in *Gaudium et Spes*, the Second Vatican Council's Constitution on the Church in the Modern World, the Council Fathers say, "everyone must consider his [or her] neighbor without exception as another self."[20] And in the afore-mentioned *Populorum progressio*, the Holy Father expressed a hope for "a world where freedom is not an empty word, and where the poor man Lazarus can sit down at the same table with the rich man."[21]

It is useful to employ table imagery in order to get a better understanding of Catholic social thought. The poor, because of their human dignity, deserve a place at the table—a fair share of food and drink for those who hunger and thirst. Working people deserve a place at the table where decisions are made that affect their livelihoods; if they have a place at the table, presumably they will have a voice in decision-making.

The unemployed deserve a place at the table—figuratively speaking, the table associated with the workbench, a place to earn a wage.

Pastors should not try to induce guilt; that is counterproductive. They should, however, cultivate consciousness—awareness—that the poor are in our midst. There are poor people around the corner and around the world. We have to care; and if we care, we have to act. That's what the tradition of Catholic social teaching expects of us.

PRINCIPLE OF PARTICIPATION

Take a moment to reflect on the various contexts within which you live your life—as a family member, a student at school or an employee at work, as a citizen, a retiree—whoever you are, whatever you do, and wherever you happen to be. In all of these contexts, Catholic social teaching would encourage you to think of yourself as a participant. Indeed Catholic social teaching would say that you have an obligation as well as a right to participate, not simply to be a passive observer. Back in 1998, as I mentioned earlier, the Catholic bishops of the United States issued a public statement that read in part: "We believe people have a right and a duty to participate in society, seeking together the common good and well-being of all, especially the poor and vulnerable."[22] This means that without participation, the benefits available to an individual through any social institution cannot be realized. The human person has a right not to be shut out from participating in those institutions that are necessary for human development. This principle applies in special way to conditions associated with work. "Work is more than a way to make a living; it is a form of continuing participation in God's creation. If the dignity of work is to be protected, then the basic rights of workers must be respected—the right to productive work, to decent and fair wages, to the organization and joining of unions, to private property, and to economic initiative."[23] It also applies to civic life in a democracy, as I explain below; without participation, a democracy simply will not work.

Consider workplace life for a moment. According to Catholic social teaching, every human person in any workplace has a right to have some say in the decisions that affect his or her livelihood; a right, in other words, to participate. To be shut out of all discussion is to be denied respect for one's human dignity. Pope John XXIII articulated the principle of participation in his 1961 encyclical *Mater et magistra* as follows:

> "We, no less than our predecessors, are convinced that employees are justified in wishing to participate in the activity of the industrial concernfor which they work. It is not, of course, possible to lay down hard and fast rules regarding the manner of such participation, for this must depend upon prevailing conditions, which vary from firm to firm and are frequently subject to rapid and substantial alteration. But we have no doubt as to the need for giving workers an active part in the business of the company for which they work—be it a private or a public one. Every effort must be made to ensure that the enterprise is indeed a true human community, concerned about the needs, the activities and the standing of each of its members."[24]

This line of thinking about participation can be applied to the family, where all family members have a right to participate in decision-making. Some, of course, have greater responsibility and authority; but all have a right to be heard.

In the Roman Catholic wedding ceremony when the nuptial blessing is given, these words, referring to the bride, are directed toward the groom, who has just become a husband: "May her husband put his trust in her and recognize that she is his equal...." She is indeed his equal and has an equal right to participate in household and family decision-making. Fuller and shared participation in family decision-making will surely enrich family life.

Even in school, especially in the higher grades and at the collegiate level, students have a right to participate in establishing what I like to call the "terms of trade." Professors, principals, and deans have the final word, of course, but they should never simply decide without some participation by students in the decisions concerning workload, tests, grading, papers, and other practicalities. Not that the student voice would be determinative, but it should be heard. And the principle of participation should nudge students in the direction of faithful, steady work, not just showing up for class and idly sitting there. Similarly, in the parish, all have not just a right but a duty to participate; passive participation is unacceptable.

The principle of participation touches upon the central element in democracy where citizens have not just the right to vote but the obligation to vote. It is a moral obligation that is all too often overlooked when Church leaders speak out on moral-political issues but neglect to remind those they are instructing on the morality of various issues in the political arena that they, the voters, have a moral obligation — first to register to vote and then to participate in the political process by casting their vote. It is both surprising and discouraging to see, after election results are in, how many citizens did not register and, among the registered, how few, relatively speaking, participated by actually casting their vote.

There is a lot more to participation than simply voting. Qualified candidates are needed to run for office. Intelligent and competent citizens have to be willing to accept appointments to boards and commissions. Their participation will advance the common good. And it is no exaggeration to say that any community is only as strong as the level of volunteer community service activity within that community is high.

Participation and information go together; one without the other is clearly insufficient. Catholic social teaching calls for both. All of us have an obligation to stay informed. I know it is an unfair question, but I used to enjoy asking students which was more important to them—their credit card or their library card. Failure to have or use a library card is not a minor matter. Just as to read nothing but the sports page in the daily newspaper is to declare oneself a borderline illiterate, never to read a good book is to abdicate responsibility for one's intellectual growth, not to mention the cultivation of the creative imagination.

Productivity in the workplace is directly proportionate to the level and quality of participation on the part of those who interact there. No single manager knows all there is to know about the business and the markets; no one person possesses all the ideas necessary to move the organization forward. By adopting the principle of participation and applying it to the way meetings are run and decisions are made, employers assure that their organizations will be both productive and profitable. This is true as well in the not-for-profit sector of organizational activity. And it applies not just to employers but to pastors as well.

At the leadership level of any functioning organization, there will typically be daily or at least weekly meetings of the leadership group. Participants should be in touch with the thoughts and feelings of all members of their respective subgroups and be able to represent those thoughts and feelings at the table when top decision-makers gather. At any level—from the top on down through the lower levels—all participants should have the opportunity to speak. Why else would they be at the table? From personal experience, I'm convinced that all such meetings should include a "go-round"—a time dedicated to speaking up on the part of all participants in the meeting even if, on occasion, a given participant chooses to say, "I pass." Sometimes an off-the-wall comment will be made, and the person chairing the meeting should never fail to ask, "Do the rest of you agree with that?" If not, the comment should be left to die a quiet death and not permitted to distract or delay progress. This is simply to acknowledge that while participation is essential to organizational health, not all participation is of equal value.

Studies have demonstrated that where participation reigns, both morale and productivity are high. Where participation is denied, discontent is widespread and employee turnover is a problem. This is just another instance of Catholic social teaching facilitating good business and organizational practice.

Return now to the context that was set for you at the beginning of this reflection on participation: namely, the various contexts within which you live your life—as a family member, a student at school, a parishioner, or an employee at work, as a citizen, a retiree—whoever you are, whatever you do, and wherever you happen to be. And reflect now on how much richer life in each of these contexts would be if the principle of participation were in evidence there. This, after all, is the aim of Catholic social teaching: to enrich human lives and strengthen society. Papal encyclicals, for example, always speak to what is traditionally known as a "social question." Countless social questions have arisen over the years. We have seen them in the economic, political, family, and other areas of life. One way of formulating the social question that applies to our time and at all times is simply this: "How can the human community of individuals, families, neighborhoods, and nations live together in peace secured by justice?" In any answer to a specific question related to that very general expression of the social question, participation will have a role to play. Hence, the importance of considering participation in the context of pastoral leadership.

THE PRINCIPLE OF HUMAN EQUALITY (JUSTICE)

The focus now will be on the challenge of communicating an understanding of justice, and I approach the challenge by considering both ideas and images of justice. Ideas of justice are familiar and plentiful: treating equals equally; giving to each person his or her due; being fair. The great tradition of Catholic social teaching provides additional ideas of justice in the form of principles. It is important to remember that principles are ideas in need of legs: they are articulated in order to prompt activity; they are intended to lead to something. Images help this process along. There is, for instance, the image the prophet Amos employed to communicate the idea of justice. Recall that prophets are not those who, as the popular imagination portrays them, predict the future. Old Testament prophets like Amos are those who point to the present injustice and warn that if corrective action is not taken, dire consequences will follow. Since more often than not, appropriate action was not taken and the consequences followed, the prophet became known as one who foretold the future (the dire consequences). Not so. The role of the prophet is to be God's voice in denouncing an evil and calling for remedial action, and being God's finger in pointing to an existing injustice. Listen then to the prophet Amos:

> This is what the Lord God showed me: He was standing, plummet in hand, by a wall built with a plummet. The Lord God asked me, "What do you see, Amos?" And I answered, "A plummet." Then the Lord said:
> See, I am laying the plummet
> in the midst of my people Israel;
> I will forgive them no longer.
> The high places of Isaac shall be laid waste,
> And the sanctuaries of Israel made desolate;
> and I will attack the house of Jeroboam with the sword. (Am 7:7-9)

This is the famous image of the plumb bob. You sometimes see them in little holsters on the hips of surveyors. Although new technology means that they are used less frequently now, they are employed by surveyors in staking out the lines and boundaries of new roads and other construction projects. The "plummet" or, as we call it today, the *plumb bob*, drops directly down from the surveyor's fingers; it is a pointed, cone-like metal weight that seeks the earth's center. The string from the plumb bob to the fingers holding it creates a vertical line—a plumb line—to be seen in the cross hairs of the surveyor's instrument, the *transit*.

Israel is going to be measured for its uprightness, its justice, says the Lord, through the voice of Amos. If the nation is not upright, if it is "out of plumb," as builders would say, it will surely collapse. Think for a moment of how we borrow from the vocabulary of the building trades to communicate an idea of justice—on the level; fair *and square; up and up; four square.* An unjust society will fall just as surely as will a wall under construction that is not straight, that is "out of plumb."

By far the best image of justice for purposes of communicating an understanding of justice is, in my opinion, the familiar scales of justice: the image of two trays in balance on a scale. You see that image everywhere.

Recall how the law is represented by the statue of a woman, tall and strong, a blindfold over her eyes, her arm extended straight in front of her, her right hand holding the scales of justice. The blindfold signals the law's impartiality to either side in a dispute. When the scales are even, justice prevails. When an unfair advantage is taken, it shows through as a downside gain taken at the expense of the upside loss. Compensatory (*pensa* is the Latin word for weights) action is called for; the weights must be rearranged so as to bring the trays back into balance, into a state of justice. You see the scales of justice as insignia on lawyers' cuff links, tie clips, and other jewelry, on desk ornaments, wall hangings, and bookends.

Apply the image of the scales of justice for purposes of social analysis. If I pick your pocket (a simple one-on-one example of injustice), my downside gain is taken at the expense of your upside loss. To make things right again, I've got to get that wallet back where it belongs— on your tray. Now think of other imbalances from the perspective of social justice, still employing the framework of the scales of justice. Look at the differences in life expectancy between African-American children and their white contemporaries in the U.S. Compare educational attainments or income distributions between selected groups. Think of compensation received in the workplace by men and women doing essentially the same work. Consider daily caloric intake in the developed over against the less developed economies of the world. Look at the balance (or imbalance) of trade between rich nations and poor.

In every case the question is the same: Is one tray's favored downside weight taken at the expense of deprivation on the other tray? There must, of course, be some relatedness if the analysis is to conclude that corrective action is required in the name of justice. The relatedness between a pickpocket and his or her victim is clear. Not so clear is the relationship between the advantaged and disadvantaged groups in the other comparisons I just made. To the extent that there is an identifiable relationship between the two, then you can begin to look for evidence that one side's gain has indeed been taken (and is still being enjoyed) because of the other side's loss. There is a clear causal connection and justice calls for remedial action. It might be established, for instance, that the imbalance is the result of prejudice, exploitation, greed, or abuse of power.

Where imbalance is evident, but a relationship is not obvious and a causal relationship cannot be established, then charity, compassion, the common good, a commitment to solidarity and social responsibility will call for compensatory action that strict justice might not be able to compel. At times, appeal has to be made to our sense of humanity if action is to be taken to correct inhumane conditions or clear wrongs that have ambiguous or even contested social origins. The problem will not go away on its own. Even if the accusing finger can find no clear target, an honest social conscience will accept the verdict Rabbi Abraham Joshua Heschel once rendered in the face of massive social injustice, "Some are guilty; all are responsible."[25] Widespread acceptance of that verdict means that some corrective action will certainly follow.

As a practical matter, justice educators and pastors should take care to distinguish ethical justice (giving to each person his or her due) from biblical justice (attending to fidelity—fidelity to our relationships to God, to the people God has placed here with us on earth, and to the care of God's creation). Reason helps us get a grasp on ethical justice; revelation, which presupposes faith, provides the foundation for coming to terms personally and as a faith community with the demands of biblical justice. There will indeed be demands.

Take, for instance, the issue of world hunger. Hunger is a justice issue. In my experience, one of the best ways of getting in touch with the hunger issue is through Bread for the World, a Christian citizens' lobby that has, for more than forty years, been an effective advocate for the hungry poor by lobbying the U.S. government's legislative and executive branches. Bread for the World's analysis of the issues is always sound; the advocacy is always sane. Both the lobbying organization, Bread for the World, and its politically neutral educational arm known as the Bread for the World Institute are located at 425 Third Street, SW, Suite 1200, Washington, DC 20024. Bread for the World began in 1974 as a Lutheran parish initiative and welcomes parish affiliations now from across the Christian denominational spectrum.

Community service, in age appropriate settings, is a great laboratory in which an understanding of justice can be (not necessarily will be) gained by students from middle school on up. They call it service learning, but the learning won't happen without on-site supervision and off-site guided reflection on the experience.

Let me conclude these reflections on justice with an observation about style. How should Catholic Christians conduct themselves while rendering community service and working for social justice? They should first become acquainted with what St. Paul, writing to the Galatians, lists as the "fruit" of the Spirit—evidence that the Holy Spirit is present in a person and that person's work: love, joy, peace, patience, kindness, generosity, faithfulness, gentleness, and self control (Gal 5:22). These quiet virtues were discussed in Chapter 1 and described as constitutive of the "infrastructure" needed for parish leadership. Paul cites them as evidence that the Holy Spirit is there, active and engaged in the effort. The same Holy Spirit is also there in the noisier virtues of justice, fortitude, advocacy, and prophetic denunciation. But an infrastructure of the quiet virtues, the nine Pauline Criteria for the presence of the Spirit, must first be in place to guarantee that it is the Holy Spirit, not the self-love and assertive ego of the advocate that is making necessary noise on the road to justice.

THE PRINCIPLE OF STEWARDSHIP

A steward is a manager, not an owner. The idea of stewardship is grounded in the first verse of Psalm 24: "The earth is the Lord's, and the fullness thereof." God is the owner of the earth and of all that it contains. The "fullness thereof," in the sense of what is grown or extracted from the earth and later refined, shaped, or fabricated, also belongs to God. You may hold a deed and legal title to your property, but the biblically based idea of stewardship says that you own nothing absolutely. Everything you own you hold in trust. You are a manager, not an owner. And your trusteeship of all that is yours—your treasure, time, and talent—means that you have a responsibility to use what you own wisely, for the glory of God and for the service of others (as one way of expressing your gratitude to God for what you have). You are also obliged to use "the earth" carefully with an eye to conservation, so that future generations will not be deprived.

From the perspective of Catholic social teaching, stewardship is a moral category. You can be a good or bad steward, faithful or unfaithful, just or unjust in your management of "the earth" and any portion of it that you might own.

On June 18, 2015, Pope Francis released a lengthy encyclical letter titled "Praise Be to You: On Care for Our Common Home." The Italian title is *Laudato Si'* (drawn from the famous canticle of St. Francis of Assisi, "Laudato si', mi Signore."). This encyclical is addressed, said the pope, to "every person living on this planet.... I would like to enter into dialogue with all people about our common home."[26] He addresses forthrightly issues of the ecological crisis, chief among them environmental deterioration, climate change, and shortages of potable water.

Not surprisingly, critics say Francis should stick to religion and refrain from pronouncements involving economics and politics. But in this case he clearly has science on his side and is advancing the entire body of Catholic social teaching by bringing a sense of moral urgency to a call for action in defense of the environment. The great Catholic tradition of social justice is at risk if Catholics and those within their sphere of influence fail to connect in the policy arena worldwide with all the great social issues of our day, not least of which are those related to the environment.

The idea of stewardship touches both the gift dimension and the moral obligation associated with people and their planet or "the land," as we often refer to it. This is not the "promised land" that I have in mind here, the land to which God calls his chosen people. I am thinking of the land as all of material creation given by God to our care and for our use. Stewardship says that everything we possess we hold in trust. The conditions of that trust are set by the Creator, who "entrusts" to our care varying proportions of material creation. An ethic of stewardship concerns itself with fidelity to, and violations of, that trust.

The unethical steward is the person who violates that trust (1) by neglecting to care for that which has been entrusted; (2) by destroying without adequate reason the substance of that which has been entrusted; or (3) by appropriating or assigning to oneself the exclusive use of that which has been entrusted, and doing so in a way which denies the legitimate claims of others. An unethical steward is one who enriches him- or herself on that which has been entrusted, at the expense of those (including future generations) for whom the trust is held. The unethical steward is characterized by insensitivity, pride, avarice, and greed. The ethical steward exhibits a character—the internal source of external behavior—that is compassionate, trust-worthy, humble, and self-sacrificing. The contradictory vices are sins or sinful tendencies to which Catholic social teaching calls attention.

It is late, but not, of course, too late for ethicists and theologians to reflect on private property as an occasion of contemporary sin and unethical conduct. This would be yet another approach to the exaggerated egocentricity which is personal sin and the collective depersonalization, damage, and disregard which describe social sin. This is a fresh approach necessitated by the evidence of sinfulness in our times (the extremes of wealth, poverty, human oppression, starvation, and the unjust exploitation of both resources and persons). Personal and social sin must be examined today through the window of private property and thus engage the principle of stewardship.

St. Thomas Aquinas regarded the institution of private property as an accommodation to the state of the human race after the fall. As one of the principles around which human societies can be organized, pri-vate property is seen by Aquinas as a form of social organization that offers a realistic expectation that property will be preserved for the service of the community. Aristotle before him noted in *Politics*: "that which is common to the greatest number has the least care bestowed upon it."[27] Reflect for a moment on your own conduct in a public park and your private garden, in a rented automobile and in your family car. Sinful human beings all, we have an ongoing moral problem in containing our disordered self-interest. As Edmund Burke once remarked, "All men that are ruined, are ruined on the side of their natural propensities."[28] Those propensities must be held in check.

Since the possession of private property appeals to our self-interest, the institution of private property represents a workable, although risky, way of preserving "the land." But preservation is only part of the task of stewardship. Sharing the land and using it for the benefit of the community require equal attention. Traditional moral analysis would grant to those in real need, and to those who have been unjustly denied access to the land, the right to override another's right of private ownership. By refusing to share, or by denying necessary access, say, to water to others in the community, or by unreasonably exploiting, for motives of personal enrichment at the expense of others, the land and those who labor on it, the private owner reveals him- or herself to be unethical in the conduct of stewardship.

Attitudinal change will be a necessary forerunner to any realization of the ethical ideal outlined here. An attitude is a tendency toward action, and behind the tendency there will always be a motive. Abundant motives are available for incorporation into a contemporary ethic of stewardship. Pope Francis' encyclical on the environment is full of them. His hope in publishing it is, of course, to get people thinking and talking about the problem and eventually arriving at the conclusion that something must be done—even if it hurts.

Environmental and ecological data are registering concern among those whose eyes (although burning perhaps) can still see, and whose ears (although ringing) can still hear. Air, water, soil, and noise pollution are outdistancing control measures. Nonrenewable energy resources are being rapidly depleted. New technology is not keeping pace; population growth in the poor two-thirds of the world and consumption growth in the affluent one-third of the world pit people against resources as well as people against people along lines of division on "the land." These emerging lines suggest that the land, if managed in a way contrary to the ethics of stewardship, has the potential in our day of becoming a battleground between rich and poor. Personal and collective self-interest perceived in terms of survival (the ultimate natural motive) would, one might expect, nudge us toward remedial or preventative action. Prior to action, however, there must be attitudinal change. We simply cannot continue the attitude that "what is mine is mine absolutely and I can do with it as I wish." Nor can we afford to continue to sustain the attitude that "my money entitles me to consume or control on my own terms as much as my money will buy." And if attitudinal change on the part of individuals is going to be difficult to achieve, just think of how great the challenge of bringing about attitudinal change on the part of powerful governments and large corporations. Nonetheless, there is reason to be hopeful.

In the secular sphere, analysts are noting a shift in ideas and attitudes that underlie our economic institutions, thus making the traditional foundations for those institutions less secure. Classical economic analysis regarded human labor (along with land and capital) as a "factor" of production. "Economic man" was presumed to act only in ways conducive to maximization of personal utility and satisfaction. Today we have all but broken away from a "value-free" economics. We see no longer an "economic man" but a human person interacting with other human persons as well as material wealth in an economic system. The system itself, regarded by all as standing in need of improvement, is seen to be a complex but consciously coordinated network of activities rather than a constellation of blind forces operating with the blessing of Adam Smith's "invisible hand." Most, but not all, who live within the United States economic system see evolution and reform as capable of shaping that system toward greater sensitivity and responsiveness to human values. Some, representing a significant minority, see revolution and replacement of that system as the only way of correcting the human disvalues and curbing the abuses of economic power at home and abroad.

The idea of stewardship is alive and well in our midst. It stands, however, in need of legs strong enough to carry us forward on the road to social justice.

THE PRINCIPLE OF ASSOCIATION

The principle of association represents an important idea in the tradition of Catholic social thought. To be clear, I'm not interested here in any psychological theories of association, free association of ideas, or anything along those lines. I'm thinking of people connecting up with other people.

"[O]ur tradition proclaims that the person is not only sacred but also social. How we organize our society—in economics and politics, in law and policy—directly affects human dignity and the capacity of individuals to grow in community."[29] Those words come from a statement of our American Catholic bishops back in 1998.

We Catholics hold that the centerpiece of society is the family; family stability must always be protected and never undermined. By association with others—in families and in other social institutions that foster growth, protect dignity and promote the common good—human persons achieve their fulfillment.

Just consider for a moment the word "socius," which is Latin for "friend." See it there in the middle of the word "association." See it as well in the word we use so often: "society." In order to develop as persons, in order to live full human lives, we need friends, we need associates; we cannot go it alone. We are social beings. Indeed we were never meant to go it alone. And in order to get where we need to go, want to go, have a right to go as human beings, we have to connect with others. Our road to progress is sometimes blocked by what appear to be insurmountable forces. To overcome those forces—especially when they are human oppositional forces—we have to team up, organize, bond together; thus bound together we can remain committed to nonviolence and still make progress. If all of this sounds far removed from the daily concerns of parish leaders, it only serves to indicate how much work remains to be done to form genuine parish communities.

A book published in 2010 takes its title from an old labor song written and sung by a union organizer named Joe Hill, who came to the U.S.

from Sweden in 1901. The song is "There is Power in a Union," and the subtitle of the book, written by Philip Dray, is *The Epic Story of Labor in America*. The Joe Hill song was set to a church hymn, and it had this message for workers:

> "There is pow'r, there is pow'r/ In a band of working
> men./ When they stand, hand in hand./ That's a
> pow'r, that's a pow'r/ That must rule in every land."[30]

Well, the Church recognizes and respects that right to organize in the workplace—to form unions in order to negotiate wages and working conditions. That recognition comes under the broader banner of association thus covering a wider swath of human activity than just the workplace, as important as that is. The Church now needs to attend to the challenge of forming people into genuine parish communities.

The centerpiece of society is the family; family stability must always be protected and never undermined. As I said above, by association with others—in families and in other social institutions that foster growth, protect dignity, and promote the common good—human persons achieve their fulfillment.

The question: "What is a family?" is making the rounds today in the public policy arena. The Catholic tradition has an unambiguous answer to this question. It will speak against same-sex marriage and can do that on firm, non-prejudicial, even nonjudgmental grounds. However, to deny human persons who are also homosexual their reasonable and genuine human rights is quite another matter and, in this area of discussion and debate, the Catholic social principle of human dignity must never be ignored.

Last time I checked, eight of the Yellow Pages in the Washington, D.C., telephone directory cover associations—literally from A to Z. They reflect an impressively broad range of human activity. Their purpose is to unite people for a purpose; essentially, the purpose is some kind of enhancement of human life and advancement of human growth.

Central to the tradition of modern Catholic social thought is "the right to organize," the right to form unions, which are associations of workers that are formed to protect the dignity of workers. The principle of association has a special place in the tradition of Catholic social thought. It must be understood, appreciated, and integrated into the value system that Catholics carry with them into the culture clash that awaits us in what commentators all too facilely call "the real world." It is the only world we have, and it is going to be a far better world to the extent that we can associate with one another, become friends with one another, unite with one another for the pursuit of objectives and goals that are themselves ordered toward the common good.

Organized labor has been on the decline in the United States over the past several decades. This is not unrelated to the decline in manufacturing employment in the U.S. There are many other factors that contribute to this decline; I'll not explore them here. But I do want to say that the labor movement has seen a potential for growth by organizing government employees and looking to the service industries as well. Within the service sector, health care is viewed by labor organizers as an area for potential growth.

This has not gone unnoticed by Catholic healthcare providers; there is a large and important network of Catholic hospitals and nursing homes in the U.S. They are often managed by religious women, and some conversations, even confrontations, have sprung up across the country between union organizers and Catholic health administrators.

All should know that on June 22, 2009, a document was released by the United States Conference of Catholic Bishops, through its Committee on Domestic Justice and Human Development, that carries the title, *Respecting the Just Rights of Workers: Guidance and Options for Catholic Health Care and Unions*. This is the product of ten years of quiet and substantive dialogue between and among leaders of the labor movement, Catholic health care, and the bishops; they have been exploring together ways whereby Catholic social teaching can influence the actions of unions and Catholic healthcare institutions "in assuring workers a free and fair choice on questions of representation in the workplace."[31]

In a foreword to the document, Bishop William Murphy, of Rockville Center, chair of the USCCB committee, says: "The starting points for the agreement were the recognition that Catholic Social Teaching holds that 'health care is a human right... both a service and a ministry... [it] is a fundamental social good that is essential to the well-being of local communities and society.'"[32] And the document affirms "'two key values: (1) the central role of workers themselves in making choices about representation and (2) the principle of mutual agreement between employers and unions on the means and methods to assure that workers could make their choices freely and fairly.'"[33] This document, says Bishop Murphy, offers "new practical alternatives" to deadlock and hostility in labor relations in Catholic healthcare.

The document clearly affirms (and both union administrators and Catholic healthcare administrators agree) that the "workers in Catholic Health Care have the right to choose to join or not join a union through a process which is free, fair, and respectful of the roles and missions of Catholic Health Care and the labor movement."[34] In effect, this is saying that both unions and health care institutions have to be at their best, i.e., live up to their values and ideals, in addressing the issue of the right to organize and the place of collective bargaining in the healthcare workplace. Neither side can lie or misrepresent the advantages or disadvantages of unionization; neither side can use outside consultants to influence unfairly the decision of workers to organize or not organize. Workers must be able to vote by secret ballot, in an election supervised by the National Labor Relations Board (or by another mutually agreed upon process) to decide whether or not they want union representation.

It is often remarked that the most effective union organizer is an insensitive employer or top administrator in a private or public organization. Those administrators who resent having unions to represent their workers should, if they want to avoid unionization, make sure that they themselves are good listeners and ready responders to the legitimate needs and requests of their employees.

Organized labor has done a great deal to protect human dignity and promote justice in the American workplace for nearly a century now. The movement is by no means perfect, but it does represent one way of applying the principle of association that will always be part of the great tradition of Catholic social thought.

As I said earlier, the principle of association has relevance far beyond the workplace. It is time for all socially conscientious persons and those who want to promote social justice to examine society in terms of the withdrawal of so many from associations of any kind. I'm referring to the return of individualism—especially of the rugged variety. We are created by God's design to be together, not to live apart from one another. We have to find creative ways of fostering and developing our ability to associate. In doing so we will make life richer for ourselves as well as for those who are neglected, lonely, alienated and, sad to say, even unnoticed in our midst. In this regard, the typical parish has its work cut out for it.

THE PRINCIPLE OF SUBSIDIARITY

This next in our set of ten principles that represent the body of Catholic social doctrine is known as the Principle of Subsidiarity. Now there's an unusual, probably unfamiliar word—subsidiarity. What does it mean?

Whenever you hear the prefix "sub," you think of down, lower, below the surface—subway, for example. A subsidy is usually thought of in financial terms; it represents assistance, a gift, a grant placed under a person or project to provide needed support. Subsidiarity suggests a lower level; it connotes support from below.

Applied to organizational life (including parish life), the principle of subsidiarity means that no decision should be taken at a higher level in the organization that can be taken as efficiently and effectively at a lower level. This is a principle that keeps government in its proper place when it comes to deciding and doing what best serves the common good. Notice that this principle works in both directions. In some cases, decisions and actions must be taken at the top because there simply is not the capacity at lower levels to decide or do those things that need doing effectively and efficiently. At other times, it is just the reverse; justice requires that deciding and doing belong at a lower level if the dignity of individual members of society is not to be ignored and walked over, so to speak, by mindless people in possession of power. As I said, this is a principle that keeps government in its place.

Listen now to these words from Pius XI's famous encyclical *Quadragesimo anno*, issued forty years after *Rerum novarum*:

> As history abundantly proves, it is true that on account of changed conditions many things which were done by small associations in former times cannot be done now save by large associations. Still, that most weighty principle [the principle of subsidiarity], which cannot be set aside or changed, remains fixed and unshaken in social philosophy: Just as it is gravely wrong to take from individuals what they can accomplish by their own initiative and industry and give it to the community, so also it is an injustice and at the same time a grave evil and disturbance of right order to assign to a greater and higher association what lesser and subordinate associations can do. For every social activity ought of its very nature furnish help [subsidium] to the members of the body social, and never destroy and absorb them.[35]

> The supreme authority of the State ought, therefore, let subordinate groups handle matters and concerns of lesser importance, which would otherwise dissipate its

[the State's] efforts greatly. Thereby, the State will move freely, powerfully, and effectively do all those things that belong to it alone because it alone can do them: directing, watching, urging, restraining, as occasion requires and necessity demands. Therefore, those in power should be sure that the more perfectly a graduated order is kept among the various associations, in observance of the principle of "subsidiary function," the stronger social authority and effectiveness will be, and the happier and more prosperous the condition of the State.[36]

The state's job is to preserve the peace, promote justice, and protect the common good. Individuals and private organizations are also expected to contribute to peace, justice, and the common good, but sometimes the problems are so large and the threats so great, only the state can meet the need.

Those who say today, for example, that the care of economic casualties and the creation of jobs should be "left to government," risk violating the principle of subsidiarity, which would allow neither decisions nor actions at a higher level of organization that could be taken just as effectively and efficiently at a lower level. This principle would push decision making down to lower levels. But sometimes government must act in the interest of the common good. There will be instances, and the economic crisis that began in 2008 is surely one of them, when government must take action if the crisis is to be addressed properly and effectively.

In our present situation of widespread layoffs, rising executive compensation, and income stagnation for those who are, so to speak, caught in the middle, new public policy initiatives are being proposed. Reflective thinkers with no ideological prejudices against using tax policy for social purposes are asking: Why can't Congress bar corporations from counting as a cost of doing business any executive compensation above a certain level, say, $1 million? The corporations could pay higher levels, if they wanted to, but it would be taxable corporate income before it became personal (and again taxable) income to the executive.

The principle of subsidiarity should also apply in private sector organizations, in ordinary workplaces, including parishes. This ties in with the principle of participation and, as is so often the case, is reducible to the principle of human dignity. Individuals are not to be ground under by impersonal, anonymous decision makers at higher levels in the organization. The parish poses a particularly challenging context for the application of this principle of subsidiarity. Parishioners, like students in school, will need help in grasping this principle. It might be proposed to them as a "principle of delegation" or a principle of "proper respect for autonomy."

The principle of subsidiarity keeps the door wide open for the generation of new ideas. Creative thinking and prudent risk-taking are expected at lower levels if our economic engines are to generate jobs and income for working people. The notion of subsidiarity, along with the principle of solidarity, introduces a moral dimension into all of this—a sense of obligation to do something to advance the common good. Entrepreneurship is, or certainly should be, ethical activity; government should encourage it. Business and government should be talking ethics when they discuss job creation. They ought to be talking the principles of Catholic social thought.

What we've been discussing here is the great tradition of social justice that is the warp and woof of Catholic social teaching. The term social justice had been part of what we call social ethics long before the publication of *Quadragesimo anno* in 1931, but Pius XI is usually credited with incorporating it into the vocabulary of Catholic social teaching. It represents a departure from classic liberalism and unbridled individualism.

A commitment to social justice serves to pull the prejudicial underpinnings out from under classic liberalism—which is not to be confused with contemporary understandings of liberal as opposed to conservative social thought. Classic liberalism was an enthronement of individualism of the most rugged variety.

PRINCIPLE OF THE COMMON GOOD

The principle of the Common Good is a justice-related idea, one that needs more attention in times of social injustice and inequality.

In its *Pastoral Constitution on the Church in the Modern World*, the Second Vatican Council described the common good as "the sum of those conditions of social life which allow social groups and their individual members relatively thorough and ready access to their own fulfillment."[37] In *Laudato si*, Pope Francis refers to the common good as "a central and unifying principle of social ethics"[38] and borrows the words I've just quoted from Vatican II to define it.

The common good is not the sum of all the individual goods, nor is it a utilitarian kind of greatest good for the greatest number of people. It involves, rather, a conscious sense of respect for all persons, an acknowledgment of the basic human dignity of everyone, and a commitment to work for the promotion of conditions in society that encourage the development of each person's human potential. This idea is related to the principle of solidarity, the notion that we are, by virtue of our common human nature, connected to one another, part of the one human family. The principle of solidarity functions, you will recall, as a moral category that leads to choices that will promote and protect the common good. We are, indeed, our brothers' and sisters' keepers, and we are obligated to act accordingly. The fact that millions of Americans are currently not covered by any form of health insurance is an issue to be considered as an assault on the common good, a blow to our sense of solidarity, and that issue is, of course, at the center of our ongoing public policy debate about healthcare finance reform.

An image that helps the individual, self-interested mind wrap itself around the notions of solidarity and common good is the image of the old-fashioned inner tube and a rubber tire. The wholeness and roundness of the tire suggests the oneness of society. Hold on to that image; it applies today to tires manufactured with the latest technology long after the inner tubes fell out of fashion. You may remember plunking yourself in an inner tube used as a flotation device in a swimming pool or on a lake when you were a child. In any case, the inner tube's potential for wear and tear—the potential for a blowout that can flatten the entire tire (remember the rubber patches on those tubes?)—serves to remind that it is in the interest of the whole tire that attention be paid to a small section in need of a plug or patch. Promotion of the common good protects the ultimate good of the individual.

Let that imagery go to work to persuade you of the oneness of society (the whole tire) and the importance to the whole of being attentive to one small area of weakness and vulnerability.

Recall that the common good is the sum total of social conditions that foster the full development of human potential. Now think about the condition of family life in America (and around the world); what about the condition of human dignity? education? housing? health care? employment? peace? the environment? overall security? All of these social conditions relate to the common good.

As I said, the "Common Good" is a catch-all phrase that describes an environment that is supportive of the development of human potential while safeguarding the community against individual excesses. It looks to the general good, to the good of the many over against the interests of the one or very few.

Everyone knows you can't tell a book by its cover. But I have to admit that the title on the cover of a small paperback prompted me to purchase *The Collapse of the Common Good: How America's Lawsuit Culture Undermines Our Freedom*. The author is Philip K. Howard, who gave this book an earlier outing under the title *The Lost Art of Drawing the Line*. The title of another of his books, *The Death of Common Sense*, suggests he is preoccupied with the possibility that

America is losing its grip on something important. This prompts me to ask in the words of Alfred Lord Tennyson, "Ah! When shall all men's good/ Be each man's rule, and universal Peace/ Lie like a shaft of light across the land?"[39] Don't look for that to happen soon, Philip Howard would reply. In his view, "any notion of a common purpose is pushed aside by obsession with personal entitlement."[40]

We are losing a sense of working together to achieve common goals and protect the common good. Behind that loss is a reluctance to identify and articulate deeply held values. If, for example, the principle of human dignity is understood, accepted as a value, internalized and permitted to function as a prompter of personal choice, the person thus prompted will defend human life and dignity wherever and whenever it is under assault. Look around the workplace and the larger community for assaults on human dignity. Try to get behind the unemployment statistics. Look at urban decay. Examine the drug culture and its economic underpinnings. Consider the neglected elderly. Ask about the physical settings within which low-income children seek both education and recreation. How about those who have no health insurance? How do any or all of these social conditions relate to the common good?

Don't forget that in *its document on the "Church in the Modern World,"* the Second Vatican Council (1962-1965) described the common good as "the sum total of social conditions which allow people, either as groups or as individuals, to reach their fulfillment more fully and more easily."[41] Let that idea seep into your understanding, as apparently it did in the mind of Pope Francis, and let it become part of the way you think and look at the world.

Another way—less abstract and far less lofty—of picturing the common good is the automobile tire analogy I offered earlier. If the tire viewed as a whole looks strong but has a cut, leak, or other point of vulnerability at just one small spot, the whole thing will soon collapse. Think of this as the "collapse of the common good." One, small, unattended point of weakness or vulnerability can lead to the collapse of the whole.

In societal terms, it is in the interest of the rich and powerful to assist the poor and powerless; they're all part of the same tire.

We Catholics have to do a better job of understanding the "tire" that is the common good and then convince ourselves and our elected representatives to do all that must be done to keep the only tire we have in good repair.

This much is sure: a better understanding of the common good will lead to improved social conditions not only in the U.S. but around the world, and thus to fuller development of human potential.

Pope Francis underscores the importance of this principle of the common good in these words in *Laudato si'*:

> "Underlying the principle of the common good is respect for the human person as such, endowed with basic and inalienable rights ordered to his or her integral development. It has also to do with the overall welfare of society and the development of a variety of intermediate groups, applying the principle of subsidiarity. Outstanding among those groups is the family, as the basic cell of society. Finally, the common good calls for social peace, the stability and security provided by a certain order which cannot be achieved without particular concern for distributive justice; whenever this is violated, violence always ensues. Society as a whole, and the state in particular, are obliged to defend and promote the common good."[42]

As we come to the end of this consideration of ten principles of Catholic social teaching, it is fair to ask: Where is the tradition of Catholic social thought going? It will always be rooted in a commitment to the recognition and protection of human dignity. It will continue to speak to issues of human life; it will encourage participation in decisions that affect human welfare. It will never abandon the poor. It will remind believers of the implications of the principles of solidarity, subsidiarity, and stewardship in their lives. It will never lose sight of the importance of promoting and protecting justice in the world, as it continues to promote the common good and foster various forms of association that are essential to the full social development of the human person. In other words, the principles of Catholic social thought will continue to serve as driving forces behind a social justice agenda into the unknown future.

There are, it is fair to say, several issues that have received insufficient attention in the past—for example, racism, war and peace, and before Pope Francis appeared on the scene, the environment. You can be sure you will be hearing more about these as the Catholic mind wraps itself around social concerns in the future.

After reviewing the sweep of interests and issues associated with the great tradition of Catholic social teaching, it is clear that parish leadership cannot be viewed as a sole-proprietor, solo-flight situation. The responsibility simply must be shared. The need will not be met unless many hands and hearts are joined; setting goals and guiding the direction of that collective outreach is the responsibility of parish leadership. Moreover, it is the responsibility of the pastor to get this process going.

CHAPTER Three

The Leadership Team

Forgive me if I seem to have taken an excessive amount of time to arrive here at an on-the-ground consideration of parish life. I don't apologize for this. Parish life in the United States today needs both a new spirituality along the lines offered in the first chapter and an awareness of the principles of Catholic social teaching, spelled out in Chapter 2. Now, with those two chapters in place and the hope that their contents will be assimilated by all who want to make our parishes better, we can move to the more familiar territory of the urban and suburban parish with which readers will be familiar. So let's begin with a consideration of the parish leadership team.

Any parish, large or small, must be organized. The organizational chart has a place (not a pedestal!) at the top, for the pastor. As in any administrative or organizational set up, the top slot marks the place where "the buck stops."

The phrase, "the buck stops here" was made famous by U.S. President Harry S. Truman, who had a sign bearing those words on his Oval Office desk. The sign was given to him by a poker-playing friend. The meaning of the expression derives from a practice in poker where a marker, called a buck, was passed from one player to another indicating whose turn it was to deal the cards. Popular usage associates responsibility and accountability with "the buck." Where the buck stops, responsibility and accountability rest.

It is useful to incorporate the expression into parish life because decisions have to be made in parishes. Someone has to deal the cards. Things have to move. This is not to say that responsibility cannot be shared; it is simply to suggest that it is the pastor's responsibility to make sure that when action is necessary, something happens; things keep moving.

THE TEAM

In a large urban or suburban parish the pastor will sometimes have the assistance of one or more "parochial vicars," ordained priests who, as needed, could take the pastor's place. We used to call them assistant pastors. Nor is it unusual now to have an ordained deacon assigned to a parish. Other positions, filled on a full- or part-time basis, will typically include: parish secretary, director of liturgy, director of music, director of religious education, business manager, and facilities manager. Other functions that may require a full-time person, or might be handled on a part-time basis or incorporated into the job description of a member of the full-time staff, are: human resources, budget, planned giving, website management, communications, youth ministry, child care, home visits, hospital ministry, and social concerns. Standing committees in the form of a parish council, finance council, and committees on education, social concerns, worship, and community relations will include persons on the payroll—full or part-time—and unpaid volunteers. The pastor has to make sure that these committees meet on a regular basis, and the pastor must be responsive to what they recommend.

A Table of Organization will emerge from the positions just mentioned. That table will, for the most part, be composed of the names of persons holding those positions. They should have a place at the table when the parish staff meets. This is the leadership team.

Given the spiritual infrastructure laid out in Chapter 1, it can be assumed that everyone who holds administrative responsibility in a given parish will recognize that the word "administration" contains within itself the word "minister" or "ministry." The parish secretary has a ministry. So do the budget director and the plant manager, no less than the music director or the director of liturgy. Failure of any member of the administrative team to see his or her work as a ministry amounts to a failure of leadership and represents a point of vulnerability on the "tire" of the common good (to employ the metaphor explained in Chapter 2). Points of vulnerability are where "blowouts" occur; they require the immediate attention of the pastor. If any point of vulnerability is left unattended, the common good of the parish will surely suffer.

There should be a weekly meeting of parish staff—same time, same place, no exceptions. Attendance is, of course, expected of all staff members. Typically, the pastor will chair the meeting. Detailed minutes need not be kept, but there should be an agenda, distributed in advance, and there should be a summary of meeting highlights distributed shortly afterwards, thus providing a record of decisions made and responsibilities assigned.

Meetings should begin and end with a prayer. It is useful to have a "consent agenda" made up of non-controversial items that are mainly informational and can be considered "without objection" right at the start. Next, action items are considered in proposal form and, after discussion, voted up or down. Part of every meeting should be a "go-round" allowing everyone at the table to report items of interest related to the area of his or her special responsibility. The go-round works best if the pastor goes last.

SPACE

Every parish has to manage space—worship space, office space, meeting space, storage space, residential space, library space, parking space—and care must be taken to make sure that space is accessible to and supportive of disabled parishioners. Allocation of space for regular use is a responsibility of parish leadership.

Typically, parishes have inherited the space they use for worship—the church building—and the residence for ordained clergy—the rectory. There may be a day way out in the distant future when parish priests (often called diocesan or secular to distinguish them from priest members of religious communities) will live in apartment clusters with shared dining and recreational facilities. They would thus have companionship, and they could use their private automobiles, mobile telephones, and other electronic devices to be ever close and always available to their parishioners but not dwell within doorbell distance from those who need their services. For the present and foreseeable future, however, parish priests will live, as most now do, in residences proximate to their parish churches. That living space may or may not include office space—best if it doesn't, but a given is a given. Whatever the arrangement, every parish priest must have a private place where he can meet parishioners seeking advice and counsel. This space must be attractive, accessible, and soundproof, where conversations cannot be overheard and outside noise will not make conversation difficult. The importance of having secure, private, pleasant office space for pastoral conversations cannot be overemphasized.

Worship space, typically a given, need not be so architecturally fixed that it cannot be adapted to help shape community. Most churches are designed to resemble theaters—rows of seats where worshippers can sit side-by-side with their attention fixed on a distant point in front of them. Such seating does not encourage them to see the faces of one another; it enables them rather to see the backs of other worshipper's necks. This can be softened a bit by turning pews at the left and right ends in toward the center, partially facing one another. This helps to encourage and foster a sense of community, assuming parish leadership has been successful it its effort to form a faith community. And the more a congregation can be encouraged to worship as a group of individuals formed into a faith community, the easier and more natural it will be for them to pray for one another.

The centerpiece of worship space should be the table altar, not the tabernacle where the Blessed Sacrament is reserved, although the Blessed Sacrament should be reserved in a tabernacle off to the side and easily accessible for private worship. Some parish churches have reservation chapels. Others have alcove-like settings where the Blessed Sacrament is reserved. "Visits" to the Blessed Sacrament are a precious part of Catholic devotional life, and sensitive architectural design will help to preserve that. In parish life, architecture should always be in service to theology, and sound theology continues to view the consecrated elements that constitute the Holy Eucharist primarily as food, as bread broken and passed around for the nourishment of the believer, not as a deity to be adored.

MUSIC

Church music by its very nature is heard, not seen, although musicians in some worship settings are sometimes up front in plain view of the congregation. This usually serves to promote congregational singing. Musicians should be good at what they do, and parish leadership should make sure that those who perform are well trained and well rehearsed.

Older churches typically have a choir loft in the rear where the organ is permanently installed and where the choir members gather to sing. In cases where the musicians—both singers and instrumentalists— assemble up front and to the side, and remain visible throughout the service, a piano or organ is usually up there with them. This arrangement makes a statement about the importance of music in supporting the worship, indeed in helping to create an appropriate worship environment. A lone organist can create an attractive worship environment.

I recall visiting a parish church for Mass one summer Sunday many years ago in Philadelphia. I noticed that the organist was softly playing the four hymns that the congregation would later sing during the liturgy; the respective numbers from the hymnal in the pews were posted for all to see. During the quiet time before Mass began, the organist was playing the melodies in reverse order from the order in which they would be sung during Mass, and the volume for the opening hymn rose nicely to bring the congregation to its feet as the celebrant approached the altar. A suitable tone had been set.

The typical parish will have an all-volunteer adult choir. Some will have a children's choir as well. Choirs need rehearsal time apart from the time immediately before worship, which should be quiet, mood setting time. Singing in the choir should be considered a form of ministry and belonging to a choir viewed with a sense of pride. What the choir sings is a matter to be discussed at the leadership level with the music director, and when the choir sings should be determined with sensitivity to congregational preferences. Some people, for good reason, prefer a quiet Mass, and often the early morning Mass on Sunday accommodates that preference.

Special attention should be paid to having appropriate music for weddings and funerals.

HOMILIES

Every Eucharistic liturgy is divided into three parts—the Liturgy of the Word, the Eucharistic prayer, and Holy Communion. The homily is an extension of the proclamation, i.e., an extension of the Word proclaimed from Scripture. It is rooted in Scripture. It represents an effort on the part of the homilist to filter the inspired Word through his own faith experience and to match it up to the faith experience of those in the congregation. This is no easy task, given the different ages, experiences, and needs of the people in the pews. This is not to say that there is never room for a topical sermon at homily time on Sunday—an address targeted on some particular external event or special need. Parish leadership has a special responsibility to make sure that silence does not prevail in the face of an urgent situation—the clergy sex abuse scandal, for example—simply because the readings for that Sunday do not easily admit of extension in that particular direction. The parish pulpit is not intended to be a "bully pulpit" for political commentary, but neither is in intended to be a shelter or hiding place when a crisis emerges.

In normal circumstances on a typical Sunday, before the readings are proclaimed, some parishes invite very young children to slip away to a special place where a leader will read Bible selections just for them and explain the meaning of the word thus proclaimed, before leading the children back to join their families for the Liturgy of the Eucharist. This helps the youngsters to feel "special," and it makes it easier for the homilist to address more sophisticated and complicated issues.

It is important that parish leadership make sure that the acoustics in the worship space are good. Can everyone hear what is being said from the pulpit? You won't know, unless you ask. If they can't hear, what's the point of preaching in the first place?

EVALUATION OF HOMILIES

When I was pastor of Holy Trinity in Georgetown, I introduced a system of brief but random evaluations of the Sunday homilies. Unannounced, there would be evaluation forms in the pews; the homilist would not know in advance. This would happen about once every quarter. The single-sheet evaluation form invited parishioners to be helpful to the clergy by answering several questions. First, they were asked to indicate by day and time (e.g., Saturday, 5:30pm or Sunday at 11:00am) the homily under evaluation; it was not necessary to know the name of the homilist; the pastor knew that. Then a check-off response was invited: The homily just heard was (1) excellent, (2) very good, (3) good, or (4) poor. Next, it could be heard (1) clearly and easily or (2) hardly at all. And by check-off identification, the respondent indicated where he or she was sitting—front right, left or center; middle right or left; rear of church right or left; balcony—thus enabling the pastor to correlate possible acoustical problems with physical locations in possible need of improved amplification. Next, a few blank lines inviting a response to this simple statement: "The point of the homily was ..." Then the evaluation form provided space for general comments completing these two sentences: "I would suggest that the homilist consider... " And "I would appreciate hearing something about _____ in a future homily."

Parishioners invariably expressed appreciation for the opportunity to express their views; they often went out of their way to express gratitude for the effort the homilist devoted to that task. The forms could be dropped into the collection basket or returned by mail to the pastor, who shared the evaluation with the homilist. Not a complicated process, but a direct contribution to the improvement of preaching in the parish.

Some might be interested in having for reference my three-volume set of Sunday homilies, all available from Paulist Press: *The Word Proclaimed: A Homily for Every Sunday of the Year, Year A*; *The Word Explained: A Homily for Every Sunday of the Year, Year B*; and *The Word Received: A Homily for Every Sunday of the Year, Year C*. This set of three books sells for a reduced price of $54.95.

Before leaving the pulpit, let me say that it is also important for parish leadership to monitor the quality of lectoring—the voice, diction, volume, and pacing of the oral delivery of the readings from Scripture. Auditions should be held before reader selection is made. Performance evaluation should be made from time to time with special attention to the pacing of delivery. Proclamation from the pulpit is not the same as conversation on the telephone. Not all volunteers are good lectors.

MONEY

When I served as pastor of Holy Trinity, I followed the example set by my predecessor, Father Larry Madden, S.J., by delivering an annual "Sermon on the Amount." There it was, once a year—full disclosure, open books—not to bore, simply to inform. How much money was received? From what sources? How much was spent? Where did it go? And since we were a "tithing" community committed to social justice, how did that ten percent of offertory income find its way to meet genuine needs under the guidance of our Social Concerns Committee? The timing of the "Sermon on the Amount" coincided with the delivery of the annual external audit of parish finances. Even though a diocesan audit might be conducted, an additional independent audit of the parish is recommended. At Holy Trinity, parishioners were always invited to inspect the audit, if and when they wanted to, in the parish office.

We were also a community of "Pledged Parishioners." Our members were invited, by a committee of their lay peers, to pledge an annual amount as offertory income to the parish. Payments could be made periodically; some "heavy hitters" simply let the basket pass them by on a given Sunday because they had already made their quarterly or semi-annual payment on a hefty pledge.

I am, by academic training, an economist and have managed money under the old "fund accounting" system at several universities where I served as president and liked to think and speak to staff in terms of four "buckets" (or funds): (1) the annual operating fund recording current income and expenditures; (2) the plant fund accounting for the value of the physical plant as well as holding funds to be spent for renovation and repair; (3) the endowment fund containing money that yielded (usually at the rate of five percent of principal) dollars to be spent for donor-designated purposes; and (4) the loan fund, a special category containing, for the most part, federal funds to be loaned to and repaid by students. For every dollar of endowment, I used to say, "We have a nickel to spend. Let's get to work and build up that endowment!"

The management challenge each year was to be able to show a positive current fund balance (a surplus) when the audit came in; it delivered a "photo finish" picture of the institution's financial health at the close of the fiscal year.

It is important to understand the distinction between an audit and a budget. The annual budget is a planning document; it rests on assumptions that are subject to external influences and might easily change. An audit, on the other hand, is an unalterable picture of how it all turned out on the final day. As the wags like to say, the auditors come around after the battle to spear the wounded.

Parish leadership should enlist the help of registered parishioners who are trained in finance and accounting and willing to serve on committees that oversee these areas of parish activity. It is foolish for a pastor to pretend that he understands all the ins and outs of parish finances when he doesn't. Help is available, if he is humble enough to ask for it. And the money needed to support the parish ministry is usually there, but will not be forthcoming unless transparency prevails. I know a pastor who stood up one Sunday and told the people that he had good news and bad news to share with them regarding an upcoming major expenditure. "Everyone agrees that the need is great and we've got the money to meet it," he said. "That's the good news. But the bad news is that all the money is in your bank accounts, not ours." Transparency in the parish office creates a welcoming environment for individual contributions—for transfers from parishioners' private bank accounts to the parish treasury.

An annual "Sermon on the Amount" can eliminate what many parishioners regard as an irritant: namely, the tendency to "talk about money" in Sunday sermons. That really isn't necessary where transparency prevails. And the fact that "talking about money" drives people away from Sunday worship is enough to activate concern at the leadership level.

SECOND COLLECTION

Another familiar practice in many parishes is the so-called second collection. There are about ten of them, give or take, in the United States each year; all but one are taken up on a Sunday (the collection for the Holy Land is taken up on Good Friday), and not all of them are taken up every year in every diocese. They occur throughout the year, but there is no firm schedule. And in some parish churches, they are taken up by having the ushers simply return to the front of the church after the regular offertory collection and then walk up the same aisle once again with their collection baskets in hand instead of waiting until after Holy Communion.

In no ranked order of importance, the designated beneficiaries of special collections are (1) The Campaign for Human Development (a domestic poverty program), (2) Catholic Relief Services (foreign aid), (3) World Missions or Propagation of the Faith, (4) The Catholic University of America, (5) Black and Indian Missions, (6) Shrines in the Holy Land, (7) Retired Religious, (8) Retired Diocesan Priests, (9) The Local Ordinary's Charities Campaign, (10) Diocesan Catholic Education.

The Catholic population of the United States represents the largest unorganized philanthropic potential in the world. Failure to organize this potential by specifying collection dates (for example, by simply designating the second Sunday of every month for a special second collection) and failure to announce the purpose of the collection clearly and persuasively in advance, as well as on the day it is taken up, amounts to a colossal failure on the part of national Church authorities. Such failures explain the loss of millions of dollars that would otherwise have been applied to very worthy causes. An occasion for this nationwide diocesan sin of omission is the common complaint from pastors that they do not want to talk about money and the collective failure of their bishops to override these complaints.

In my view, it is the responsibility of the bishops to agree on the ten special needs or causes that deserve national Catholic support. They should then assign one need to the second Sunday of each month, and reserve the month of November for diocesan Catholic charities and the month of December for a special parish need. There you have the twelve months covered and the beginning of the formation of a Catholic mindset that links second Sunday to special need.

SPECIAL FUND RAISING

Parishes have a lot to learn from both for-profit and not-for-profit organizations when it comes to fund raising. For instance, one well-known and highly successful private university president, who has raised millions of dollars for Catholic higher education, likes to say, "It's the heart that gives; the fingers just let go."

Pastors can translate that into a good fund-raising principle that says in effect — preach to the heart, minister to the heart, and be sure to appeal to the heart when there is need for money to keep the ministry going. The "giving heart" will respond not just when the basket is passed, but also in reflective estate-planning moments when the parish or parochial school is named as a beneficiary in the grateful parishioner's will.

While they are still among the walking "wellderly," some parishioners, particularly widows, widowers, and unmarried seniors, who have no immediate dependents but live in homes that are mortgage free, can be approached in a businesslike way by members of the parish finance committee and asked to will their homes to the parish with an instruction to sell the property and apply the amount realized through the sale to an endowed "chair" for one of the parish school teachers, an endowed scholarship for the school, an endowed position on parish staff, or a special fund to support weekend religious education, adult education lectures, or a special outreach fund to help the poor.

To create an atmosphere that encourages this kind of thinking, any pastor can take a page from the corporate playbook and produce an annual report, as Holy Trinity Parish now does, in the form of the annual "Sermon on the Amount" given at all Masses on a given Sunday. Full disclosure of dollars received and dollars spent is the best way to demonstrate transparency, which, in turn, builds both loyalty and confidence in the hearts of those who can and will write the checks.

Lay expertise can be enlisted to set up a computer-based system for (1) assessing each parishioner's potential to give, (2) scheduling lay participation in face-to-face requests for "pledged" annual gifts to help finance parish operations, (3) tracking the record of giving, (4) recording acknowledgments of all pledges and special gifts, and (5) reporting, in the spirit of good stewardship, the performance of any managed funds, as well as expenditures of designated gifts for designated purposes.

On a national scale, better organizational planning would significantly enhance fund-raising effectiveness in the American Church, as it does for National Public Radio, the United Way, and so many other secular causes. If, as I indicated earlier, "Second Collection, Second Sunday" could become a reality, it would eliminate the need to "talk about money" much beyond a simple announcement. A week before, diocesan newspapers and parish bulletins could carry a well-reasoned and worded "case" for the special need, written by professionals associated with the beneficiary organization.

Where a diocese has television contact or radio outreach to Catholics, word about an upcoming collection can go out in the preceding week. Posters, Power Point presentations, flyers, envelopes, and any other explanatory material that would focus attention and highlight the need could be sent in advance to all the parishes by the beneficiary office or organization.

As I mentioned above, U.S. Catholics represent the largest unorganized philanthropic potential in the world. Improved organization would make a philanthropic world of difference.

THE PARISH TELEPHONE

What follows immediately in this section first appeared as a brief essay that I wrote for the newsletter that Villanova's Center for the Study of Church Management sends on a quarterly basis to parishes across the country. Like any business, a parish should want to be "customer friendly" and readily responsive to telephone inquiries. This means no undue delays in having a call answered, and, if the call triggers a recorded welcome, a mercifully brief "menu" of press-button options on the way to contact with a live voice at the other end of the line.

Many businesses include "response time" in the set of metrics they use in their normal efficiency measures for meeting customer needs expressed in phone calls. Reduction in the time a caller has to "hold" is always desirable. Measuring response time is possible with available telephone technology.

Sometimes a live voice at the business end receives the call, and then one of several actions (not all customer friendly) follows: (1) "Hang on," is one of the less elegant instructions; (2) "Please hold," is always better to hear, unless it means being shunted off to soundproof isolation; (3) the "hold" status may be accompanied by soft music, a tune-in to the radio news, or recorded advice on the benefits of exercise—none of which is tolerable for extended periods; or (4) the exasperating experience of having your request heard but not acknowledged; you are simply switched to another line that may or may not be related to the object of your original inquiry. Obviously, this is not a good telephonic way to initiate dialogue or open a transaction in any business or any parish.

Callers to some parishes get the Sunday Mass schedule (which can be extensive) before hearing a live voice or other recorded options. In some cases, callers hear a live voice identifying the parish, giving the receptionist's name (often inaudibly), and asking "How may/can I help you?" when a simple, "Hello, welcome to St. Malachy's" would do just fine.

When a nationally known business was having problems with the quality of its "hotline" customer service, one of its top managers decided to investigate. He learned that as a result of insufficient training, the customer service representatives were not answering calls promptly. Here's how a business writer describes the situation: "This caused the caller to be in an irate mood by the time the call was eventually answered, resulting in a confrontational conversation and further dropping the morale of the employees at the call center."[43] So the supervisor "placed a mirror in front of each telephone operator and beseeched them to look into the mirror before and during the call. He asked them to make sure that their facial expressions were friendly. It was a simple move, but it achieved the desired result."[44]

If every pastor put a mirror in front of each rectory phone (including his own) what wonders might be worked in the cultivation of improved parish relations!

KNOWN BY NAME

Parish leadership has an ongoing challenge to learn and remember the names of individual parishioners. Instead of simply admitting defeat at the outset and acknowledging that it can't be done, the good leader will give it a try. Typically, a photo album can serve as a foundation for this ongoing effort. Have the camera ready at all times in the parish center or in the back of the church and assign someone the editorial and custodial responsibility. Identification by face and name is essential, by home address helpful. Having a photo taken should be part of the registration process in every parish.

We all enjoy being known and called by name. Just by calling their priests "Father," the laity act as if they know their clergy by name. The priests are not so fortunate. It takes work, but it is worth the effort. "Hello there" just doesn't do it.

Some parishes, typically small ones (and more often Protestant than Catholic), use name tags to help parishioners get to know one another by name. This is a praiseworthy goal; whatever works to bring it about is worth considering. Replacement on a rack in the back of the church at the end of the service is the system used by some. No system will work, however, unless the people are willing to cooperate.

In the early twentieth century, it was common to have a "block collection" once a year in every Catholic parish. This was before urban sprawl. Typically, row or semi-detached homes were arranged block by block; certain streets marked the parish boundaries. Territorial parishes were common; parishioners tended to live within walking distance of their parish church. The point of the block collection was more to get to know the people than to raise money for the parish. Those days are gone, but the need to get to know the people remains. How to meet that need remains a challenge.

Parish priests should be visible around the church building, inside or out, before and after Sunday Masses. Greeting is part of their job description. Politicians do this during campaigns leading up to Election Day; priests should be doing it all year round. Greeting the people is another way of blessing the people.

Think of the interesting things that just might happen if a parish priest decided to get into his car every day, drive to a predetermined block, park and walk around the block, and then return to the rectory. Repeating this ritual every day would eventually enable him to cover the entire parish. It would also enable him randomly to meet some people on their own turf, not his, and to associate family names with streets. The Holy Spirit works in random ways. Surely, some of these encounters would be the work of the Spirit bringing pastor and parishioner together in unexpected ways. This "out and about" strategy can be an effective form of parish leadership. Modern living does, of course, leave many neighborhoods deserted during the day—not all, but many. Early evenings and weekends may provide the best "out and about" opportunities. We won't know unless we try.

Underlying all this is a principle of inclusion, a belief that everyone counts and should be included; this is a scripturally grounded and theologically-sound conviction that "we are one."

It is helpful to look back over the American Catholic experience of parish life historically and sociologically to better understand where we've been and where we now are with respect to the principle of inclusion. In the old days when the "Sunday obligation" reigned supreme, any parish could count on having a captive audience every Sunday. Not to be there was to risk eternal damnation, so the people showed up often as passive spectators to what was happening around them in a language and ritual they did not understand. Aware that they had a captive audience, preachers were not overly concerned about "holding" their hearers and, regrettably, often went into the pulpit poorly prepared. In those days it was a "sermon," not a "homily" that was part of Sunday Mass, and sermons were not of uniformly high quality. Nonetheless, the people showed up. That is no longer the case. People are showing up irregularly, if at all. And this is a contemporary challenge for parish leadership.

CHAPTER Four

A Place at the Eucharistic Table

The reason for existence of any parish is to provide a place at the Eucharistic table for members of a faith community who want to be present there. Parish leadership will make sure that the table is in place, that it is attractive and accessible, uncluttered by anything that could distract the gathered faithful from the realization that this is the place where the Lord is remembered in the breaking of the bread and at this table they are invited to give praise and thanks to God. I alluded to this in the previous chapter when I listed space considerations as having a place on the parish leadership agenda.

There is a much quoted passage in the *First Apology* of Justin Martyr that can serve to take us back to our earliest days as a faith community and provide perspective on what we should be doing now to foster and promote Sunday worship. Justin wrote this in the year 150:

> "On the day called Sunday, all who live in the city or the outlying districts gather together in one place. The memoirs of the apostles or the writings of the prophets are read, as long as time permits. Then, when the reader has ceased, the president of the assembly verbally instructs and exhorts all to imitate these good things. Then we all rise together and pray, and when our prayer is ended, bread and wine are brought forward, and the president offers prayers and thanksgivings to the best

of his ability, and the people assent by saying Amen. Then there is a distribution to each of that over which thanks have been given. And to those who are absent a portion is sent by the deacons. Those who are well off give what each thinks fit; and what is contributed is kept in the custody of the president to be given to orphans and widows and those who are in want, and in bonds, or strangers sojourning in our midst; in a word to all who are in need. Sunday is the day on which we hold our common assembly because it is the day when Jesus Christ our Savior rose from the dead."[45]

There they are—all the familiar parts of the Mass as we know it today: the readings, the homily, the Eucharistic prayer of thanksgiving (made, before the invention of print, to the best of the presider's ability!), the congregation's approval expressed as a collective "Amen," the communion, and the collection of money for subsequent distribution to those in need. These elements have been there from the beginning. Parish leadership has to make sure that the table is in place today in attractive architectural and artistic surroundings along with a presider who is prepared and ready to serve.

As we all know, they are staying away in droves these days—nominal Catholics who choose not to attend Mass most Sundays of the year. When you ask them why, you get replies ranging from awful homilies to poor music, unwelcoming congregations, exclusion of women from priesthood, aloof—even "arrogant"—clergy, mismanagement on the part of the hierarchy of the clergy sex abuse scandal, and on down the line to an "I-just-don't-get-anything-out-of-it" explanation.

Over the past few years, I've been studying the decline in Sunday Mass attendance in the Catholic community. Some I've talked to recall what we used to call the "Sunday obligation" and say they just don't worry about the heavy penalty that catechized Catholics have been taught is attached to willful omission of that obligation. It was a capital crime, a mortal sin, they were taught as children. They don't believe that makes much sense anymore.

In the old American vernacular, "much obliged" was a way of saying "thank you." In searching now for a persuasive nonthreatening way to explain how the Church (which, as we know, opposes capital punishment!) wants us to understand the Sunday obligation, it might be good to reflect on the old American vernacular.

"Much obliged" means thank you. It is an expression of gratitude. And what the Church expects of its members on Sunday—Resurrection Day, the first day of the week—is a formal liturgical expression of thanks. That is the Sunday obligation. Eucharist means thanks doing, thanks saying, thanks giving.

At Sunday Mass, we give thanks for the gift of our salvation through the death, Resurrection, and ascension of Jesus. Not to meet this obligation—not to offer praise and thanks—is to be an ingrate. Moreover, we give thanks in community, not as isolated individuals, because that's how we've been ransomed, that's how we've been saved—in community. And finally, we do it in the Eucharistic community because the Eucharist, a thanksgiving ritual, forms us into the one Body of Christ.

Many good Catholics mention when they go to Confession that they "missed Mass on Sunday" because they were sick, or taking care of others who were sick, or traveling and not able to get to church, or otherwise indisposed. They didn't do anything wrong; they do not need to confess missing Mass. "It just makes me feel better if I mention it." That's understandable, but it is also an indication of scrupulosity and immaturity. The question to ask is, given those impeding circumstances, did you take some time to give thanks, to express gratitude, even though you were unable to do so at Mass? If you failed in this regard, you probably have an insufficient understanding of the Sunday obligation.

Some people have to work and are thus impeded from being present for Mass. They can consider themselves excused, but they should seek from a confessor a dispensation from the obligation, although the confessor will surely advise them to get to Mass on another day of the week.

The problem that we have not yet openly addressed is the right of the bishops (not individually, but in council) to attach the "pain of mortal sin" to the failure to observe the Sunday obligation. They appear to have done that in the Third Plenary Council of Baltimore in 1884, and they do have that right. But sin remains a matter of personal choice in the face of three conditions: serious matter, sufficient reflection, and full consent of the will. And this points to the need now for the bishops formally to withdraw the "pain of mortal sin" penalty they attached to the failure to go to Mass on Sunday and to offer persuasive and clear explanations of the reasons for the obligation. (While they are at it, they might mention that they used to teach that it was a mortal sin to eat meat on Friday. Not all obeyed that rule; what happened to those sinners when they died?)

Another window on this whole question is the notion of entitlement—the idea that we deserve everything we have, that in some unexplained way—on our own—we earned all that we possess. We are deserving, not gifted. We have no need of saying thanks; or so we seem to be thinking, at least unconsciously. The sense of entitlement is shaping contemporary culture.

Through the window of entitlement, we can see pride where we did not previously notice it; we might even begin to understand that ingratitude is at the root of all sinfulness. And the shock of that recognition may wake us up to the importance of the Sunday obligation. This is all part of the work that the bishops have to do today. They will want to recognize a distinction between influence and control and resist invoking controls when their efforts to influence are losing ground.

Meanwhile, all of us have to confront the fact that we do not want to be seen as ingrates in the eyes of the Lord. Some who are no longer going to Mass on Sundays may be willing to admit that they are sinners;

WILLIAM J. BYRON, S.J.

nobody's perfect. But ingrates? There's a question that they have to confront with care, and the teaching Church has to be creative and persistent in bringing that question to the attention of all the faithful.

This will not be easy in an era far different from that of the 1880s when the Third Plenary Council of Baltimore felt compelled to come down so heavily on this issue. They exercised poor pastoral leadership. The bishops could and should do better today. What a pleasant surprise it would be if at any time soon the bishops decided to mark the annual celebration of the Feast of Corpus Christi (the Thursday after Trinity Sunday) by withdrawing the penalty of capital punishment they attached back in 1884 to failure to attend Sunday Mass.

For some Americans, Corpus Christi is simply the name of a city in Texas. For Catholic Christians it is (or should be) the centerpiece of their worship, the central reality of their religion, the Body and Blood of Christ present in sacramental form, given as food and drink for nourishment on a continuing journey of faith. The Bible recalls how God fed the Israelites with manna in their forty-year exile in the desert (Exodus 16: 4-36). It was, in effect, their day's food for their day's march while in exile. And so should be the Eucharist for the modern Christian—at least the week's food for the week's march in faith. In St. Paul's first letter to the Corinthians, you will read: "Is not the cup of blessing we bless a sharing in the blood of Christ? And is not the bread we break a sharing in the Body of Christ?" (1 Cor 10:16) Indeed they are!

We Catholic Christians have the Blood and the Body of Christ in our midst, at the table. The Eucharist is here to transform us, as St. Paul put it, "Because the loaf of bread is one, we, though many, are one body for we all partake of the one loaf" (1 Cor 10:17). This is remarkable sacramental, supernatural reality—on our altar, in our midst, shaping us into the one Body of Christ here on earth!

In the sixth chapter of the Gospel of John, we have what I like to think of as a "homily" on the Eucharist delivered by Jesus, in anticipation of the institution of the Eucharist, and occasioned by the miraculous multiplication of the loaves and fishes that you can read about in the same chapter. That miracle story is a familiar one. Did you ever speculate that the miraculous multiplication of the loaves might have prefigured the multiplication of the real presence of Jesus in the consecrated elements of bread and wine in the sacrament of the Eucharist? In any case, listen to the "homily" that those who constructed the Gospel of John put on the lips of Jesus as he declares himself to be the Bread of Life: "I myself am the living bread come down from heaven. If anyone eats this bread, he shall live forever; the bread I will give is my flesh, for the life of the world" (Jn 6:51).

Those are absolutely astounding words. Imagine if you were in the crowd gathered there and heard these words for the first time. You may have been like those in the crowd whom the Gospel describes as quarreling among themselves and asking: "How can this man give us [his] flesh to eat?" (Jn 6:52) The Gospel continues with a further explanation, an explanation supplied by Jesus himself: "Let me solemnly assure you, if you do not eat the flesh of the Son of Man and drink his blood, you have no life in you. He who feeds on my flesh and drinks my blood has life eternal, and I will raise him up on the last day" (Jn 6:53). Astounding claims! Critically important instruction! And then Jesus concludes this "homily" on the Eucharist with these words: "This is the bread that came down from heaven. Unlike your ancestors who ate [the manna] and still died, whoever eats this bread will live forever" (Jn 6:58). Absolutely astounding. Profound. And we take it all on faith!

Thank God for the gift of faith that is yours. And thank God for the gift of the Body and Blood of his Son that comes to the table of the altar to feed you, to nourish your faith. Without faith, Scripture, including this passage from the Gospel of John, is an unlighted torch. With faith, you can read and hear the Gospel, and see—with the eye of faith, to be sure, but see nonetheless—your way to eternal life. Your way is safe and secure because it is in him, and with him, and through him, who is the Corpus Christi whom we adore and celebrate throughout the Catholic world.

Parish leadership should pause and look around. Why are the pews not full? How can human creativity be applied to the challenge of making the parish church become what sociologists call a "third place" in the lived experience of parishioners? Third place is a sociological category that marks the next most important living space, after home and workplace, for most of us. I'm not talking about winners and losers when I refer to third place; I'm talking about human connectedness. And I'm raising the question because I think it is important for pastors to see that there is a lot of work to be done in making their parishes a "third place" magnet in the lives of their parishioners.

We connect primarily in the home. In order to make a living, we connect in the workplace. But there is a lot more to life than home and work and that more—as in the case of family life and work life—is usually associated with connecting with others in some identifiable place.

For many the "third place" is the club, or entertainment complex, or some cultural or recreational center. It could even be the local barber shop. John Mackey, co-CEO of Whole Foods Market, boasts of establishing tap rooms inside his stores as a third place for customers. Beer on tap is available for immediate consumption there in the middle of the store. "The new venue was hugely successful from the day it opened, with very strong sales and high profit margins. It turned out that customers identify Whole Foods Market (as they do Starbucks) as a 'third place'... where they enjoy hanging out."[46]

Typically, a parish has no pull on the loyalties of parishioners except for weekend worship, although the parish does have the potential to provide socialization—a sense of community—as well as gathering and meeting space for a variety of activities that can make lives fuller and more meaningful.

Church planners have to begin thinking of how the space under their control—the physical space that they own—can be used not only for meaningful liturgies, but also to attract members of their faith community to a fuller experience of social life. Some have parochial schools that add vitality to the place Monday through Friday. All could have libraries with associated lectures and discussion groups. Some have "job seekers" support groups. Others have sports leagues, potluck suppers, dances, young adult groups, child care, adult day care, and a variety of other activities that go well beyond the after-Mass coffee-and-donut gatherings on Sunday mornings. But none of this will work if the people have no desire to come together. They won't come together if they don't know one another. And they will surely not come together unless they are summoned out of their isolation in creative ways. This will not happen without the on-the-scene presence of a welcoming pastor assisted by welcoming volunteers. Hence pastoral planning has to begin with the people. What do they want? Who will lead? Who will open the doors and turn out the lights?

The pastor surely cannot do it all. But only the pastor can initiate a strategy for providing a "third place" option in his underutilized space for those who are looking for company and something to do. He'll be surprised to find how many who fit that description are already registered on his parish rolls. He might also be surprised to learn how little they know about the Eucharist and how it, on the table in the parish church, can be a magnet capable of drawing and holding them all together as a faith community.

CHAPTER Five

Gratitude in Parish Leadership

Gratitude is a prototypically Catholic characteristic and is, in my view, central to our Catholic identity. I've said it often and would argue the point anytime, that if I were pressed to reduce the entire meaning of religion to one word, that word would be gratitude. The case for making that one word "love" instead of "gratitude" is worth attempting, but I recall learning from the First Letter of John that it was God who first loved us, thus enabling us to love—by his good gift of love—and therefore all we can be is grateful. Why? Because he first loved us; he graced us. "In this is love: not that we have loved God, but that he [first] loved us and sent his Son as expiation for our sins" (1 Jn 4:10).

I am also fond of reminding anyone who cares to listen, as I did in Chapter 4, of the old American vernacular used to express gratitude by simply saying, "Much obliged." Obligation under God springs from a sense of gratitude. Acknowledge gratitude as your only stance before God, and you begin to notice the presence of moral obligation to do or not do certain things that God wants you to do or avoid.

There is a multiplier effect associated with gratitude, and the wonder of it all is that gratitude can, if you let it stretch your mind, magnify your happiness.

I once knew a small time politician who was constantly being bothered by people looking for jobs in city government. "Six people want the job," he told me, "you get it for one and wind up with one ingrate and five enemies." Success and security can make ingrates of us all. That's more than a bit strange, but nonetheless true. Perhaps it is saying something about self and selfishness, or it may simply be spelling out a little lesson in human nature. Human nature does have an insular, self-enclosing, self-interested tendency. Perhaps that relates to the survival instinct. But human nature is also social, and relational, outward reaching, needing to link and bond. But will human nature share—naturally? Not easily and perhaps not naturally, but it would be simply erroneous to contend that sharing is unnatural when human happiness depends on it. So we have to learn to share. And we learn through various stages of growth and the development of our sense of gratitude. The closer you get to open and generous sharing, the clearer the signal you are sending to others that gratitude is driving your decisions. It is critically important, therefore, for parish leadership to be characterized by gratitude. I mentioned earlier one pastor's good advice, namely, "Spray the place with praise;" I would repeat that now in the vocabulary of gratitude: Never tire of saying, "Thank you." This should be neither unusual nor difficult in a community organized around the Eucharist.

There are stages in anyone's degree of growth in gratitude, in showing oneself to be "much obliged." The higher you rise above a childish "avoid getting caught" morality to a principled "doing the right thing" stage—doing it regardless of who notices and without consideration of any reward except knowing that you did the right thing—the more refined your sense of gratitude is.

Gratitude is the ground of moral obligation and being grateful is the best way of declaring your dependency on God. Count your blessings and be thankful. St. Ignatius of Loyola, founder of the Jesuit Order, once remarked that he saw ingratitude as the root of all sinfulness.

A contemporary Jesuit told me recently that he is convinced that a grateful person cannot also be sad. His point is that gratitude and unhappiness cannot coexist in the same person at the same time.

So, if you are unhappy, take a moment to check on your gratitude quotient. You may be suffering from a serious gratitude deficit that will, upon examination, explain your unhappiness.

So it is important for leaders to think about gratitude, even pray about it. The title of my 2006 book, published by Paulist Press, is *A Book of Quiet Prayer*.[47] Toward the end of that book you'll find these words designed to serve as a starter for any reflective person thinking about giving thanks to God.

> I could start counting now, Lord,
>> and I would be at it for days taking inventory
>> of your blessings to me.
> Forgive me for not noticing them more readily
>> and more often.
> When everything is going well, I rarely think of
>> pausing to say thanks.
> That's simply wrong of me and terribly immature.
> Now that I am taking a moment to think about it,
> I'm beginning to notice the arrogance in my refusal
>> to say thanks and the selfishness of putting myself
>> on center stage without a nod to playwright,
>> producer, and supporting cast, not to mention the
>> folks who built the theater and sold the tickets.
> Let me shun for this brief moment the spotlight I
>> crave in order to find the humility I need.
> And there, on the ruins of my self-centeredness,
> I pray for an abiding sense of gratitude. One word
>> turns my heart to you: Gratias!

I recall helping a man prepare for death not long ago. He was a successful editor and author. He was battling terminal cancer at age seventy-one. He asked me to sit down and talk to him about it—What would it be like? How do you say goodbye? How could he make it less sad and difficult for his wife? He reminded me that he was a reporter and wanted to "cover" his own story, so would I mind if he recorded our conversation?

One thing that struck him in that conversation, he later told me, was the central religious significance of gratitude for the believer. I had said to him something like, "Just let yourself repeat the word "gratias;" breathe it in and out. Say it to God, of course, but say it to those around you too." And I suggested that he think of "gratias" as a blanket that he could pull up and around him there in bed. "Wrap yourself in thanks," I said. And he did, so that he could die gratefully even if, as most of us humans, he wasn't altogether grateful to be dying.

Albert Schweitzer once remarked that, "At times our own light goes out and is rekindled by a spark from another person. Each of us has cause to think with deep gratitude of those who have lighted the flame within us."

That is a most constructive exercise—good for the soul as well as for human relations: "to think with deep gratitude of those who have lighted the flame within us." I always tell students who are applying for college, or graduate or professional school, not to fail to mention in their personal essays those others (usually elders)—teachers, coaches, mentors, relatives, friends—who helped them along the way. Lifted their sights. Challenged them to use their talents. Perhaps even lighted the flame when fear or discouragement had set in.

I underscore that point by telling them what a member of the admissions committee at a front-ranking law school told me. She reads the personal essay first, and if there is no mention made of anyone other than the applicant—i.e., no mention of a role model, a sacrificing parent, a helpful coach or teacher,—then this reviewer would just set the application aside because, as she told me, she didn't want to have anything to do with adding more self-centered people to a profession that already had more than enough self-interested, self-enclosed members in its ranks. And what she does is not unfair, she says, because if the applicant is really strong on all other measures, the applicant will be accepted.

Here is another story about gratitude that goes back many years to a summer Sunday when I was working at Fordham University in the Bronx in New York City. I took the train from Fordham Road up to White Plains to visit with friends. They were to meet me at the station in White Plains and take me to their home for the afternoon and evening. So when I arrived, I walked through the station and, on the way, noticed a man that one might call a drifter, or hobo, or, as some used to say, a "knight of the road." He was sitting on a bench inside the station and our eyes met briefly as I passed by. I greeted him with a simple hello and went outside. A few moments later, I noticed him coming up to me outside the station. I instinctively reached into my pocket for some coins, but he waved that off and said, "No I don't want any money; I just want to thank you. You're the first person who has said anything to me in the last two days!"

Even when you are down on your luck and have very little, you can still say thanks!

I would urge the reader to review the past twelve months. You should be able to find a lot of gratitude prompters there. First, express gratitude for the gift of life and grace, and for the gift of faith. Then continue on down the list of the many reasons you have to be grateful. This is a healthy exercise at any time.

I want now to move this reflection off in another direction, although at the end of this brief excursion, I shall arrive back at the notion of gratitude.

On the Sunday before Pope Benedict XVI arrived in the United States in April, 2008, *The Philadelphia Inquirer* ran a positive editorial of welcome and took the occasion to raise an interesting question: "What does it mean to be a Catholic in the U.S. today?" This is an important question, and the range of possible answers is wide. No one respondent can say it all, but all thinking Catholics should try to form a reasonably concise reply. I would begin by saying that being a Catholic today means being a person of commitment within a community.

The community, of course, is the Church, with the pope as leader, teacher, and symbol of unity. But within the Church we find ourselves in other communities. There is the conjugal community for so many (marriage and the family). There are celibate religious communities for some, and there are those who remain single but still belong to families and relate to others in a variety of helping relationships.

Countless Catholics identify with other communities in their workplaces and in leisure hours where they are known as Catholic and where they witness to the truths of their Catholic faith.

The commitment associated with being a Catholic (remember, I said that being Catholic means being a person of commitment within a community) is, first and foremost, to Jesus Christ. We are Christians. Catholic life is Christo-centric. It is both nourished and celebrated in the Eucharist. The community within which this commitment is most evident is a worshipping community that remembers the Lord in the breaking of the bread (Acts 20). Being Catholic means being part of all that through both Word (Scripture) and Sacrament (we Catholics count seven of these). Being Catholic also means having special reverence and respect for Mary because she is the mother of Jesus.

Scripture introduces the Catholic to law (the Ten Commandments as well as the law of love). Scripture, as proclamation, invites the response of faith. And Catholic faith, in search of deeper understanding, applies intellect to the content of Scripture in the exercise of Catholic theology. Theology attempts explanation, as contrasted with proclamation, and therefore develops over the years new understandings (development of doctrine). Hence being a Catholic means being lifted through life on the wings of both faith and reason.

Being Catholic also means being committed to the care of those in need. Those three C's—commitment, community, and care—say a lot about what it means to be a Catholic today.

To be a Catholic today certainly means to be with and for the poor. It means to promote peace and justice, to protect and respect human life from conception to natural death, and to care for the earth. Stewardship, in the Catholic view, extends to the care and cultivation of one's personal gifts of body and mind.

For Catholics, sexuality is to be expressed within the context of community (marriage and family, and preparation for both) as well as permanent commitment (fidelity). Sexual pleasure is purposeful in keeping with God's plan for creation. Similarly, material possessions are to be managed within the context of community (our traditions says that ownership may be private but use is common) as well as commitment (to stewardship, service, and the good of others).

Being Catholic today means having freedom, responsibility, and accountability—freedom in the Holy Spirit, responsibility for one's free choices, and accountability for one's actions and the use of one's talents A reflective reading of Scripture reminds the Catholic that (1) "you shall know the truth and the truth will set you free" (John 8:32); (2) that each is indeed his or her "brother's [and sister's] keeper" (Genesis 4:10); and (3) that all of us will have to give an account before God in keeping with the judgment scene portrayed in Matthew 25. Earlier in Matthew's gospel (5:1-12), the Beatitudes provide a summary of Catholic convictions.

Finally, and now we are back where we began, to be a Catholic means to live in gratitude for all of God's gifts, a gratitude that provides a firm foundation for moral obligation. We present ourselves as "much obliged" (grateful) before God on Sundays. And on all seven days of the week, we consider ourselves obliged as well to love one another as Christ has loved us.

CHAPTER Six

The Servant Leader

Referring to himself as the "Son of Man," Jesus explained that he came not "to be served but to serve and to give his life as a ransom for many" (Mt 20:28). For me, this provides a scriptural home for the idea of servant leadership although the original notion of servant leadership is not based in Scripture. It originated with Robert Greenleaf, a Quaker, whose book bearing that title is a classic. He was inspired, he says, by the character Leo in Hermann Hesse's novel *The Journey to the East*. In the novel, Leo is a guide on a mythical journey. Early in the journey, the guide refers to "the law of service" and says, "He who wishes to live long must serve, but he who wishes to rule does not live long."[48]

As the story unfolds, the guide disappears and the group loses its way. Leo emerges again toward the end of the story, not as guide, but as leader and titular head of the Order that sponsored the journey. It turns out that he was in fact the leader while he was in service to the group as their guide.

Robert Greenleaf was a vice president of AT&T when he first read *The Journey to the East*. He was also a student of organizations and a consultant to businesses large and small. He carried with him into his practice of management and consulting the image of Leo, the servant leader, and over the years Greenleaf came to conclude that:

a fresh critical look is being taken at the issues of power and authority, and people are beginning to learn, however haltingly, to relate to one another in less coercive and more creatively supporting ways. A new moral principle is emerging, which holds that the only authority deserving one's allegiance is that which is freely and knowingly granted by the led to the leader in response to, and in proportion to, the clearly evident servant stature of the leader. Those who choose to follow this principle will not casually accept the authority of existing institutions. *Rather they will freely respond only to individuals who are chosen as leaders because they are proven and trusted as servants.* To the extent that this principle prevails in the future, the only truly viable institutions will be those that are predominantly servant led.[49]

In his book, Greenleaf runs individuals and institutions through the servant-leader filter. He covers businesses, foundations, churches, universities, and some other not-for-profit organizations. He gives a lot of attention to trustees as servants. His view on the distinction between oversight and management of organizations will be for some controversial, but, correctly understood, his point about more direct involvement by trustees (or, in the case of business, directors) in managing the organization's affairs is not all that wide of the mark. I've served on many boards—universities, schools, hospitals, insurance companies, a bank, a presidential commission, and a lot of community-based not-for-profit organizations—and I know that, generally speaking, boards are insufficiently alert and active in meeting their oversight responsibilities. The on-the-scene CEO and his or her chief financial officer tend to control the flow of information and both the formulation and implementation of on-the-ground policies. Does any of that ring true for the typical pastor?

BEWARE THE TOP OF THE PYRAMID

Greenleaf's book cobbles together articles and papers prepared for delivery to various audiences, and he is annoyingly anonymous when it comes to identifying the organizations he is discussing. In his chapter "Servant Leadership in Business," for example, he mentions that the statements that comprise the chapter were delivered, "one to a general audience and two addressed to specific businesses,"[50] but he does not identify the businesses. I learned from a friend, who works full time for the Greenleaf Center for Servant Leadership in Indiana, that it is quite likely that the businesses were the Olga Company and either Delta Airlines or Royal Dutch Shell. I can't say for sure.

Since 1950, I've been a member of the Society of Jesus (the Jesuits) and, in 1961, was ordained a priest of the Roman Catholic Church. Knowing that, please now read along with me the following paragraphs from *Servant Leadership*:

> To be a lone chief atop a pyramid is *abnormal and corrupting*. None of us is perfect by ourselves, and all of us need the help and correcting influence of close colleagues. When someone is moved atop a pyramid, that person no longer has colleagues, only subordinates. Even the frankest and bravest of subordinates do not talk with their boss in the same way that they talk with colleagues who are equals, and normal communications patterns become warped.... The pyramidal structure weakens informal links, dries up channels of honest reaction and feedback, and creates limiting chief-subordinate relationships that, at the top, can seriously penalize the whole organization.

> A self-protective *image of omniscience* often evolves from these warped and filtered communications. This in time defeats any leader by causing a distortion of judgment, for judgment is often best sharpened through interaction with others who are free to challenge and criticize.[51]

Abnormal and corrupting? Greenleaf is not saying that this has to be the way; he is simply suggesting that there is a high probability that the lone chief at the top will be out of touch and thus less effective as a leader. Given my background as a Catholic priest, I naturally thought of the pope when I first read the words I've just quoted, and I winced at the scenario Greenleaf lays out. It prompted me to reflect on the organizational structure of my church. I accept that structure, of course, but I recognize that it is staffed by human beings and that they are subject to the weaknesses, foibles, and failings that Greenleaf observed in his study of organizations.

In Catholic circles, whenever an ordinary priest is "elevated" from the ranks and made a bishop, he is likely to receive a congratulatory note from a priest friend who reminds him that he'll never have another bad meal, nor will he ever hear the truth again! The humor carries with it a hint of truth. Those called to serve as bishops have to remember that they walk on feet of clay and rely on the power of prayer and sacraments to protect them from the dangers of earthly ambition and corrosive pride.

Some bishops view themselves as "little popes," and, failing to understand the shepherding nature of their episcopal role, they attempt to rule rather than lead the "flock" that has been entrusted to their care. That simply doesn't work, and it is regrettable that the bishop is often the last to notice.

Insensitive presidential leadership in higher education is by no means restricted to Catholic colleges and universities, but the Catholic setting probably influenced the choice of words of a frustrated academic vice president in a Catholic university who described once for me his priest–president as being afflicted with a "bad case of the infallibles." The same affliction can affect parish leadership.

I surely don't want to give the impression that I'm out to beat up on the Catholic clergy; I just want to acknowledge that those of us who love and live in a hierarchical church should welcome the self-imposed discipline of servant leadership as protection against the temptation to forget an important principle articulated by Jesus, our Leader, who described himself, as I indicated at the opening of this chapter, as coming among us "not to be served, but to serve, and the give his life as a ransom for many" (Mt 20:28).

THE IMPORTANCE OF STAYING IN TOUCH

Extensive research on leadership styles in business has produced this sobering conclusion: "[T]he higher up the ladder a leader climbs, the less accurate his self-assessment is likely to be. The problem is an acute lack of feedback."[52] This has frightening implications for leadership in Catholic church circles.

Straight across the hierarchical board, not just in religion, but also in business, the military, the corporation, and virtually every other form of organizational life, there is a clear and constant danger of the leader being out of touch. That means being cut off from needed information and honest criticism. And in complex organizations, it is rare that one person has thorough knowledge of all the complicated parts of the whole. Every leader needs expert advice and, it goes without saying, he or she has to be humble enough to accept it.

Some readers of the *Houston Chronicle* were surely surprised to find servant leadership as the recommended solution to corporate arrogance seen by that newspaper as the cause of the economic meltdown troubling the nation at the end of 2008. "The American public has had it with arrogant leadership," said the Chronicle (December 13, 2008), which then suggested that business take "a quick U-turn from the greed-is-good model and beat a retreat to the tried and true, the ancient and honorable notion of servant leadership."[53] The editorial mentioned Robert Greenleaf and tied his seminal 1970 essay back to its ancient roots.

CHARACTERISTICS OF SERVANT LEADERSHIP

Larry Spears is executive director of the Greenleaf Center in Indianapolis, Indiana. He understands servant leadership; his center is dedicated to the "keeper-of-the-flame" mission of explaining it and facilitating the adoption of servant-leadership principles in contemporary organizational life. In his introduction to a book of essays on Greenleaf's contribution,[54] Spears identifies the following ten characteristics of servant leadership:

1. Listening. This involves "a deep commitment to listening intently to others." Servant leaders are able to get at and clarify the will of a group because they "listen receptively."

2. Empathy. This means accepting and recognizing people for "their special and unique spirits," assuming the "good intentions of co-workers," and becoming "skilled empathetic listeners."

3. Healing. Quoting Greenleaf, Spears writes: "There is something subtle communicated to one who is being served and led if, implicit in the compact between servant-leader and led, is the understanding that the search for wholeness is something they share." A leader's ability to heal is "a powerful force for transformation and integration."

4. Awareness. Being acutely aware of what is happening around him or her, as well as being in possession of a refined sense of self-awareness, is a necessity for any leader. It can be unsettling at times to see yourself as you really are and to see the problems that loom large around you, but this can be managed if the leader is also emotionally well-balanced and has him- or herself comfortably in hand.

5. Persuasion. Positional authority does not confer leadership; the ability to persuade does. "Servant-leaders seek to convince others, rather than coerce compliance." Leaders are consensus builders.

6. Conceptualization. This is the visionary function. Leaders "must think beyond day-to-day realities." "Servant-leaders must seek a delicate balance between conceptualization and day-to-day focus."

7. Foresight. "Foresight is a characteristic that enables servant-leaders to understand the lessons from the past, the realities of the present, and the likely consequence of a decision for the future. It is deeply rooted within the intuitive mind." If you unpack the first of those two sentences, you will have a training agenda for the would-be leader, namely, (1) the duty to read history (and thus become familiar with "the lessons from the past"), (2) an obligation to stay current with developments in the news (in other words, to stay abreast of "the realities of the present"), and (3) to cultivate a capacity for reflection by pondering "the likely consequence of a decision for the future." Attention to all three of these points will lead to a mastery of both the art and the science of intuition, and thus to an essential quality of leadership.

8. Stewardship. When applied to leadership, the idea of stewardship means that the leader is not an owner, but more like a manager who holds both position and property in trust for the good of others. The leader is entrusted with the care of resources—human, natural, and forged or fabricated—resources that constitute the organization. And the leader guides the use of all these resources with an eye to the common good. Stewardship involves a commitment to the service of others.

9. Commitment to the growth of people. "Servant-leaders believe that people have an intrinsic value beyond their tangible contributions as workers. As such, servant-leaders are deeply committed to the personal, professional, and spiritual growth of each and every individual within the institution." Admittedly, this sounds idealistic, but not to be missed is the link between this kind of commitment of leader to led, wherever it exists, and the loyalty and productivity that will come from followers fortunate enough to experience this kind of leadership.

10. Building community. "Servant-leadership suggests that true community can be created among those who work in businesses and other institutions. Greenleaf said: 'All that is needed to rebuild community as a viable life form for large numbers of people is for enough servant-leaders to show the way, not by mass movements, but by each servant-leader demonstrating his [or her] own unlimited ability for a quite specific community-related group.'"

These ten characteristics summarize the idea and the movement that originated in the mind of Robert Greenleaf many years ago. If understood and internalized by would-be leaders today, they can shape the future of leadership across the board in organizational life. If taken seriously by all who participate in pastoral leadership in the Catholic Church in the United States today, especially priest-pastors and bishops, they could revolutionize contemporary Catholicism.

There is a book with a curious title—*The Art of Woo* (I'll explain it in just a moment)—that offers no evidence of familiarity with Greenleaf's work or with the idea of servant leadership. Yet it belongs in the hands of any would-be servant-leader. "*Woo*" is an acronym for "winning others over." "So what is Woo?" ask Richard Shell and Mario Moussa in their introduction to *The Art of Woo: Using Strategic Persuasion to Sell Your Ideas*. "It is relationship-based persuasion, a strategic process for getting people's attention, pitching your ideas, and obtaining approval for your plans and projects. It is, in short, one of the most important skills in the repertoire of any entrepreneur, employee, or professional manager whose work requires them to rely on influence and persuasion rather than coercion and force."[55] The authors are professors at the Wharton School of the University of Pennsylvania and co-direct the "Strategic Persuasion Workshop" that is housed there.

I've made the point earlier that leadership equates with influence and requires persuasion. It is clear that command-and-control is dead and that coercion and force have no place in the pastoral leadership tool kit; strategic persuasion clearly does. As Larry Spears put it in summarizing Robert Greenleaf's philosophy of leadership, "Servant-leaders seek to convince others, rather than coerce compliance."[56] The "Art of Woo" helps show the way. And it goes without saying that the spirit of servant leadership is a treasure waiting to be discovered by those responsible for parish life in the American Catholic Church.

CHAPTER Seven

Looking to the Year 2050

An invitation from the British Province of the Society of Jesus to speak at a "Directors of Work Conference," in Oxford, England, on November 5, 2004, gave me a great opportunity to do some forward thinking. Those thoughts are included in this book because they bear directly on the larger question of pastoral leadership in the Church today. Back then, in 2004, I was asked where would the Society of Jesus be in the year 2050? What would the Church look like at mid-twenty-first century? What might an American experience of Church and change offer for consideration to like-minded Jesuits and their lay colleagues in the United Kingdom? What might the British experience have to contribute to the planning mix in North America?

My presentation was intended to serve as a discussion paper for the consideration of Jesuits and others interested in the question of Jesuit recruitment, and also for Jesuits and lay colleagues interested in the future of Jesuit works. It is relevant here because it highlights leadership issues that are going to be with us long into the future.

By way of pre-note I offered to the Oxford audience of Jesuits and lay colleagues a premise, a suggestion, a favorite quotation, and a verse from Scripture.

- My Premise: You cannot predict the future, but you can choose a future; at least you can choose some characteristics of the future you would like to have.

- A Suggestion: In his history of the first Jesuits, John W. O'Malley, S.J., points out that "one of the most striking features of the early Jesuits is the wide variety of people to whom they ministered, including many of the poor and outcast."[57] He also cites Jerome Nadal as being insightful on the Pauline characteristic of our ministry. Shortly after the death of Ignatius, Nadal wrote in his personal journal: "The Society has the care of those souls for whom either there is nobody to care or, if somebody ought to care, the care is negligent....This is [the Society's] dignity in the Church."[58] O'Malley says that for Nadal, "the Jesuit task par excellence was to search for the 'lost sheep'—whether pagan, Muslim, heretic, or Catholic."[59] In summing up, O'Malley again quotes Nadal, who wrote: "'Paul signifies for us our ministry.'"[60] So my suggestion was: read St. Paul to discover clues to guide your reflection and choices about the substance and style of future Jesuit ministries.

- The Quotation: "The Society of Jesus formally lives on its trust in each of its members. Each day in their life is a hundredfold appeal to their independence and energetic sense of duty, to their free good will, to their high-hearted love of Christ." (Peter Lippert, S.J., who entered the German Province in 1899, worked as a writer and radio commentator, was a frequent contributor to *Stimmen der Zeit* and author of several books; he died at age 57 in 1937. John Courtney Murray, S.J. used the Lippert quotation in Murray's address given on the occasion of the seventy-fifth anniversary of Woodstock College in 1944.)

- Scripture: From the Book of Deuteronomy (30:19-20), "I have set before you life and death, the blessing and the curse. Choose life, then, that you and your descendants may live, by loving the Lord, your God, obeying his voice, and holding fast to him." [This familiar "choose life" text is part of the First Reading for the Mass of St. Ignatius Loyola on July 31st.]

In our collective desire to choose life, I told the Oxford audience, I think we have to begin with some assumptions about the Church in the year 2050; what might the Church be like at the midpoint of the twenty-first century? We then should attempt to identify some elements of competence that will be needed to serve that Church (competencies that are therefore desirable, at least in potential, in candidates now entering the Society of Jesus). As I opened this up, I acknowledged my own incompetence to identify and interpret the signs of these times in Great Britain with any precision. Later in the presentation, I would speak along parallel lines to the signs I then saw and still see in the United States.

I offered, as one man's opinion, a description of what Jesuit commitment might look like in the future we can hope for, and listed some strategic conclusions relating to vocation promotion and recruitment of Jesuits in the USA, while opening the door to reflections on Jesuit recruitment in the UK.

My opening emphasis on Jesuit recruitment is not at all an indication of disinterest in the recruitment of lay colleagues for Jesuit works, nor would I want to exclude lay voices from this conversation about the recruitment of Jesuits. Quite the contrary. The point, however, that I hoped to emphasize is that we do want more Jesuits; we want more bright, holy, generous young men to enter the Society and to be there with the lay colleagues we also hope to attract to commit themselves to Jesuit works.

We know we have to be careful with respect to what we pray for—and ready to work to get that for which we pray. So discernment—personal, community-wide, province-wide, and even wider—is necessary if we are to both pray and work for what God wants to send our way in response to our prayers and efforts for vocations to the Society of Jesus.

ASSUMPTIONS.

I numbered the following assumptions for easy identification and to encourage additions, subtractions, substitutions, and deletions as others articulated their own assumptions about what the community we call church is likely to become over the next fifty years. My focus was primarily on the Catholic Church USA, distinct but not apart from the Church universal. But I acknowledged that international-mindedness will be a characteristic of American Jesuits and that service in other countries and cultures will be expected of them. And I invited all to think, as I moved down this list, of the alternate or additional assumptions others would regard as appropriate for our conversation about the Jesuit future in the UK.

1. Lay presence and influence will continue to grow in the institutional life of the Catholic Church USA.

2. The clerical culture will diminish but not disappear; the episcopal component of that culture will continue to display an inability to differentiate influence from control. (American bishops tend to believe that in order to have more influence, they have to have more control).

3. The promotion culture within the hierarchical structure of the Church will persist and thus continue to foster ambition, which, if not moderated by a spirituality of servant leadership, will continue to be corrosive within the Catholic community.

4. Optional celibacy for diocesan priests will become part of Catholic life within two decades from now, thus easing what is perceived to be an imminent "priest shortage." [Note that I made that prediction in 2004, so the "within two decades" time frame probably needs extension.]

5. Women will continue their rise in positions of responsibility and influence in the institutional Church and could perhaps find ordination an option open to them by the year 2050. If women are ordained, there will be no priest shortage in the USA.

6. Catholic participation in interfaith marriages will continue to increase.

7. Religious literacy among Catholics will continue to decline.

8. The Catholic population will continue to increase in the USA, more by immigration than by conversion or birth into Catholic families.

9. Educational attainment and family income of USA Catholics will, on average, continue to rise, but family size will not.

10. Catholic representation in positions of political and business leadership will increase.

11. Catholic education at all levels — primary, secondary, higher — will remain strong but enroll a relatively small portion of the Catholic population in those three student-age groups.

12. Catholic representation in positions of intellectual leadership, although not insignificant, will be less than proportional to their numbers in the general population.

13. Catholic influence in literature and the arts will not be particularly strong.

14. The influence of Catholic moral theology on sexual behavior and on medical and life-science experimentation will not be great.

15. In the context of a widening gap between rich and poor in the world, Catholics in the USA will not differ significantly from other Americans in their concern for social justice.

Many more assumptions can be listed. Jesuits and lay colleagues acknowledge (and respect) the fact that each person is the world's leading expert on his or her own opinion. Different opinions will generate additional assumptions, which, in turn, will contribute to the production of better conclusions about preparation for and delivery of Jesuit service to the Church in the year 2050. To offset the possible misperception that all this is too narrowly American, I repeated that I'm assuming an international-mindedness in Jesuit recruits and I wanted the audience to state the assumptions that apply best to the Church in the UK.

COMPETENCIES.

Here, in my view, are the talents and skills that I think Jesuits will need in order to be effective ministers to the Church USA in 2050. I realize that the Lord has a penchant for writing straight with crooked lines and uses the lowly to confound the proud. I know that the distribution of talents, in God's gracious providence, is uneven, and I certainly acknowledge that calling men to the Society is God's work that will be done in God's wise ways (with a wisdom that is not of this world). But there is no reason for us not to try to attract (not simply hope for, but attract) the very best talent to our ranks.

I'm convinced that anyone whom God calls to Jesuit life can become very good in the exercise of at least one ministerial skill. I should make clear that I am not ignoring in this consideration the vocation of the Jesuit brother, those who are not called to Holy Orders but are called to be vowed religious in the Society of Jesus. Brothers will have ministerial opportunities in the future that they did not have in the past; they will also have opportunities to excel in practical, secular pursuits related to the Society's changing mission to a world in need of help. Nor, to repeat, am I unmindful of the need to attract non-Jesuits to Jesuit works if those works are to survive, much less prosper in 2050. With that said, let me suggest that candidates for admission to the Society now should have:

1. The potential to become competent, even outstanding schoolmasters, professors, scholars, pastors, and preachers.

2. The potential to develop skills for: teaching, preaching, researching, speaking (in more than one language), writing, listening, community organizing, and giving spiritual direction.

3. The potential to become expert in spiritual discernment and the personal assimilation and apostolic application of the Spiritual Exercises.

4. Demonstrated ability to live and work well with others.

These competencies are rather general; within each category there is need for early assimilation of skills and, with the benefit of coaching and practice, the perfection of these skills to a high level.

I asked the audience to hold my feet to the small fire I ignited with my opening suggestion about St. Paul being a model for Jesuit ministries. You will recall the words of Nadal: "Paul signifies for us our ministry." Keep that in mind in considering all that follows.

COMMITMENT.

Commitment is a characteristic that every Jesuit must have. I would expect a candidate for entrance into the Society to be committed to:

1. Celibacy.

2. Locating oneself personally within the Paschal Mystery— i.e., to living "under the banner of the Cross" with the certain hope of participation in the Easter victory, and therefore living as a man of hope.

3. Serving the Holy See through obedience to superiors in the Society, and with this, a commitment to work anywhere in the world for the greater glory of God.

4. Helping others (our founding documents said, "helping souls," and we would now say, "being men for others").

5. It goes without saying (although Peter Lippert said it well) that there is an ongoing commitment to Christ (a "high-hearted love of Christ").

STRATEGIC CONCLUSIONS.

Now to bring this down to the level of practical choice and strategic planning, I point out first that strategic planning begins with strategic thinking, and strategic thinking has to begin with the question: What sets us apart?

We Jesuits are men on a mission. We need carefully, prayerfully, and collaboratively to discern the needs we want to be missioned to meet, or, to put it another way, the direction in which our mission is to move. What set us apart historically was a conscious desire to serve where others were not serving, to meet needs, to "help souls," to do what others could not or chose not to do. It is up to us to decide now what will set us apart in future decades.

Being the best at what we do in meeting new opportunities or unmet needs in the world that our assumptions say awaits us is consistent with our founding vision. It is up to us now to "choose life" and to honor the trust the Society has placed in each of us and upon which the Society "lives," to use the word that Peter Lippert chose to use.

Choosing life for us, it seems to me, will mean:

1. That the Society will admit to the novitiate only those who are conscious of themselves as men called to celibacy.

2. That Jesuits should work as a team, although teamwork will be more akin to performance on an American baseball team rather than other sports teams, because baseball requires individual execution of specific skills (e.g., batting and pitching) in the company of, but separable from (and even substituting for) other members of the team. It is also a game where pitching twenty wins in a

season or getting hits only one out of three times at bat is considered excellent performance. (There is a good lesson in that for Jesuits—those of us who worry about men leaving our ranks, those of us who inevitably strike out with some regularity, and those who won't do the practice needed to develop their apostolic skills.)

3. That Jesuits should live in companionship with one another but not at the price of removal from others whom the Society identifies as those to be served.

4. That Jesuits should have mobility but recognize at the same time the value of an institutional base.

5. That given the rise of both presence and influence of lay men and women in the institutional life of the Church, Jesuits should be willing to relinquish managerial control of institutions and apostolates to lay leadership, preferring for themselves positions of influence in direct (e.g., teaching and counseling) and indirect (e.g., research and writing) service to others. Hence there will be less urgency about preparing Jesuits for administration (allowing, however, for those who have the talent and want to use it in administration to do so) and more attention paid to preparing Jesuits for internal governance.

6. That Jesuit poverty should balance the need for witness to Gospel simplicity with the need for access to the tools necessary to do one's work, acknowledging that the need to give practical witness of Gospel values remains a challenge in an age of affluence for the privileged minority of the world's population in which we, for the most part, find ourselves.

7. That the catechesis of children (favored by St. Ignatius) might be revived in two forms in the USA: (a) Jesuits not otherwise committed pastorally on Sunday mornings

might volunteer as instructors in parish Religious
Education programs for parishioner children enrolled
in non-Catholic schools; (b) Jesuits could offer one-on-
one religious education for "children" who are no longer
young but living in retirement communities and nursing
homes, and whose religious literacy will likely be low.
This might be an innovative way to recapture part of
The Society's original commitment to catechesis.

8. That every Jesuit will feel obliged to respond as best he
can to the challenge Father General Pedro Arrupe gave
us shortly before he died: "The first thing that all members of the Church, bishops as well as priests and lay
people, expect from Jesuits is that they give the Exercises.
This is the primordial task of the Society."[61]

Choosing life will not be easy for Jesuits of the early twenty-first
century, but it can be done and it certainly has a lot more appeal
than the alternative.

I mentioned that Alfred North Whitehead once offered with approval
this definition of a professor—"an ignorant man thinking." So I said
to my British audience, "If you have found insufficient evidence of
ignorance thus far in this presentation, just wait to hear my impres-
sions of contemporary Church life in the UK." But that, of course, was
why we were there—to discuss the future of Jesuits works in service
to a changing Church in the UK. My ignorance needed the corrective
balance of their observations and the direction that their assumptions
could give to discussion of the future style and substance of the Jesuit
"brand" as well as Jesuit works in the UK.

My American Jesuit confrere the late Robert Drinan wrote an opinion
column regularly for the lay-edited U.S. weekly, the *National Catholic
Reporter*. Knowing that I would soon be in England, I read with more
than casual interest his piece in the September 24, 2004 issue of NCR.
It appeared under the following headline: "The Melancholy Mood

of English Catholics." Father Drinan's impression was gained from spending the month of July 2004 in London teaching a group of law students from Georgetown and several other universities.

His column paid customary respect to Cardinal Newman, Francis Thompson, Gerard Manley Hopkins, and Graham Greene before acknowledging his disappointment "to witness the gloom, even a certain malaise, in the English church." Fr. Drinan went on to say: "The Jesuits seem to have a form of depression over the fact that the centuries-old Campion College [not to be confused with Campion Hall at Oxford] closed, *The Month* magazine ceased publication, and vocations are few. The jubilation of the 'second spring' in the restoration of the Catholic hierarchy memorialized by Cardinal Newman is a memory that seems to have no echoes at the moment."[62] Most in my audience disagreed. Indeed, their Oxford meeting succeeded in "stirring up or waking up those echoes."

There were, however, signs of hope noted by Fr. Drinan. Among them were liturgies at Farm Street (the famous parish in London), the "creative and resourceful" relationship between Heythrop and the University of London, and, although not a Jesuit enterprise, *The Tablet* was, in Fr. Drinan's view, a "universally respected" publication.[63]

The negatives listed by this foreign observer represented opportunities for new ventures and future growth; if not growth in absolute numbers—of Jesuits and Jesuit works—at least new vitality in Jesuit activities. We all agreed that wishing won't make it so, but believing can have a lot to do with making it happen.

A more accurate and persuasive influence on my understanding of the contemporary Church in Britain came from David G. Barker's remarks at a lay-sponsored "Leadership Roundtable" meeting on "The Church in America" that I had attended at the Wharton School of Business at the University of Pennsylvania in June 2004. Mr. Barker was born in the UK, received his early education from the Marists, is an economics graduate of the University of London, and holds a doctorate in social administration. His career has been mainly in the management of charitable trusts.

THE CHURCH IN GREAT BRITAIN.

David Barker's remarks at the Wharton School were based on a four-year study of the Catholic Church undertaken by the Queen's Foundation at Queen's College, Birmingham. The aim of this study was to assist the hierarchy address the problems of "authority, governance, relationships, and participation in the Church in Britain." Not surprisingly, as the findings make plain, the study focused on problems, not achievements. And the problems are:

1. The "Laodicea Problem," a problem of complacency. In suggesting that the majority of British parents no longer value the transmission of religious faith to children, Barker quotes Jesuit moral theologian Fr. Jack Mahoney as saying, "the British are possessed of a vague religiosity which should not be probed too far."

2. The "Legacy of Dependence." Until fifty years ago, said Barker, British Catholics were a "defensive religious minority" living in a closed social world "in which priests held power and the laity were," he quotes from D. Ryan's *The Catholic Parish*, "... pious, moral, docile, obedient— and passive. The ideal Catholic was the child."[64]

   Still a minority (only 10 percent of the population), British Catholics, according to Barker, are assimilated into the majority population and share majority values. Not unrelated to this value shift, he noted that Mass attendance had fallen by 50 percent; priestly vocations had dropped by 60 percent in thirty-five years, and with the average age of bishops and priests rising, the clergy had been finding it difficult to relate to young people.

3. Changed "Attitudes to Authority." Barker said that individual conscience has displaced external authority as a source of moral judgment. People "seek authenticity, demand credentials, and want competence" from those in authority. British Catholics are also demanding accountability. And Mr. Barker quoted with approval Fr. Timothy Radcliff, former Master General of the Dominicans, who echoed Thomas Aquinas in saying, "The authority of the Church ultimately has to rely upon the truth of what we say—but truth born of lived experience." I suggested that our closer collaboration with the laity extends our Jesuit reach into the desired lived experience; in other words, we have new eyes with which to see, new voices to attend to in our planning councils, and broader experiences than we could otherwise have had on our own.

4. Changing Social Values. Dr. Barker pointed out a mismatch between dominant values in Britain today—"autonomy, equality, openness, empowerment, participation, tolerance, protest"—and the dominant values operative in the Church relative to laity, especially women, "as dependent upon the power and authority of an exclusively male priesthood."

5. Priesthood. Describing the Council of Trent's understanding of a priest as "a man set apart, celibate, and saintly," Dr. Barker used Professor Eammon Duffy's words to see that concept as "slowly collapsing under the joint pressures of theological and social change. [Hence there is] an urgent need to re-imagine the ordained priesthood as the counter reformation re-imagined and re-invented it." Meanwhile, the Church in Britain is experiencing what Barker described as (1) a sense of loss in the passing of the old order, and a weakened morale among its priests; (2) "a middle management gap caused by the defection of many able pastors," and (3) a curious situation in which

seminarians, who are being attracted by the dominant (but fading) ecclesiastical culture, are men who "do not relate easily to either their peers or parishioners." [I'm not sure whether by "peers" he means seminarians who are ready to adapt to something new, or to lay Catholics of their own age. He probably means both.]

I learned from Dr. Barker that the Church in Britain numbers, in round figures, about five million Catholics in 3,300 parishes; that there are about 3,000 schools and colleges, including ten seminaries. There are some 38 bishops, 7,000 priests and deacons, about 7,000 nuns, and 200 brothers, but he could offer no accurate estimate of the number of lay employees. I have no financial data.

According to Dr. Barker, British Catholics respect the person of the pope, bishop, and priest. The people "are typically loyal, concerned and supportive of the persons [of pope, bishop, and priest], but they are "out of sympathy with the institution." They find much of Church teaching "impersonal, insensitive, out of touch, lacking compassion for those in difficult circumstances and sometimes in conflict with their consciences. They are dismayed by poor communication and scandalized by inaction and secrecy in cases of abuse."

There is a poor sense of mission in the Church in the UK, according to Barker. "British Catholics have a very poorly developed sense of the diocese as the local church and of its *Mission*," said Dr. Barker. "Indeed, the diocese is frequently seen as remote, inefficient and irrelevant to their lives." Why is this the case? Because the parish is the focus of Church life and parishioners have little or no active engagement with their diocese. Moreover, "the authority of the bishop has been eroded both by social change and by centralisation in Rome.... Dioceses are geographically too large and sub-culturally too complex for the *communio model* to work effectively."

Disengaged, uninvolved, passive, unaware of diocesan priorities, spiritually unawakened, uninterested in faith development—this is Barker's broad-brush portrait of the British Catholic laity. And the discouraging picture is compounded by resistance to pastoral reorganization.

No small challenge for Church leadership. No dearth of opportunities for a creative apostolic Jesuit response. But, if Barker is to be believed, the stimulus for change for more than a decade has been externally driven, not the work of Church leadership. "Changes in the Catholic Church in Britain which promote human well-being have not been pastoral or theological," he said, "they have been driven by the demands of the Civil Authorities. The dioceses have had to respond to government policy rather than offering courageous leadership."

The areas of change that he has in mind relate to: (1) "The Charity Law Reform Acts and Employment Legislation" calling for a complete review of diocesan accounting, financial stewardship, and administration; "Education Acts" resulting in significant changes in admissions procedures, curriculum design, financial management, and measure of attainment in Catholic schools; (3) "Social Policy Legislation" has influenced diocesan child protection policies, provision for the disabled, and the functioning of diocesan welfare programs. What appears to be the case is that the state, not the Church, is advancing an agenda that might have been prompted by Catholic social teaching, if that body of doctrine had been communicated. Or, it is possible that the prompting for these changes came from public officials who had indeed been influenced by Catholic social thought. I just don't know.

Given these changes, however, Dr. Barker finds a distortion in the allocation of human resources in diocesan curias. Professionals have been recruited in the change areas, but no corresponding developments have taken place to strengthen departments responsible for pastoral strategy. Finances are setting pastoral priorities. The Church, he says, "is not an exemplary employer," and is deficient, as an employer, in human relations skills.

ISSUES AND CHALLENGES.

Finally, here is a list of "issues and challenges" with which Dr. Barker ended his assessment of the Church in Britain at the beginning of the twenty-first century:

1. The church has to learn to live with change while remaining optimistic and "having the courage to speak the truth... and the charity not to collude with injustice."

2. The institutional culture of the church has to change from fear and secrecy and control, to openness, dialogue, and co-responsibility.

3. The Christian vocation needs redefinition, and priesthood needs reinvention.

4. Attention must be paid to the theology and reality of the local church. "Bishops must take courage, acknowledge the current irrelevance of the diocese to Catholic life, and reclaim their legitimate status as the dynamic focus of the local church."

5. Needed now above all are faith, hope, and optimism. "I wish to emphasise that, for many if not most Catholics, the difficulties they experience do not detract from their faith and commitment to Jesus Christ."

This leaves us with lots to think about, pray over, and discuss on our way to deciding *where* the Lord wants us (Jesuits and lay colleagues) to move and *what* the Lord wants us to do. The challenges in the UK are not all that different from the challenges in the USA.

Wherever we are in the world, we Jesuits know that our experience of the Spiritual Exercises contributes to whatever it is that "sets us apart." We have a "substance" in faith and a "style" in our Jesuit way of proceeding. We know that the Society holds us Jesuits responsible for the "service of faith and the promotion of justice." And we welcome lay collaboration in that mission. We also welcome our Jesuit call to assist lay Catholics in meeting their emerging mission of service in the Church. All of us have to help one another.

All of us—Jesuits and lay colleagues—will have to deepen our bonds of friendship "in the Lord" while making the choices that will keep us faithful to our shared vocation.

I ended my Oxford presentation by sharing a reflection I had the foresight to bring along on the trip; I found signs of its continued relevance as I walked the streets of London for several days before moving on to Oxford for the conference. Many years ago, when I was a summer editor at the Jesuit weekly *America* magazine, Father Thurston Davis, the editor, gave me a tear-sheet from *The [London] Sunday Times Magazine* (May 27, 1962) and asked me to write a short editorial comment. I don't still have the comment, but I put the article in my files. The page-wide, single-word headline reads, "LONELINESS," and here are several paragraphs from that article:

> "You don't notice them. Loneliness is a disease without physical symptoms. Only the victims know they suffer it: the bleak sensation of walking alone through a world of other people's friends. There is no clear sign of loneliness in the pretty girl idly window-gazing in the High Street, alone; the middle-aged shabby women lingering in teashops, alone; the dark, scattered figures in the Sunday afternoon cinemas, each alone; or the old men and women who blossom suddenly on park benches in the first spring sunshine, to sit waiting and watching for conversation, alone. You don't notice them, but there are more of them now than there have ever been.

> "The number of lonely people in Britain has been rising steadily for the last twenty years. Today, general practitioners, psychiatrists, and social workers recognize it as an alarming iceberg of social malaise, in a country

which is becoming steadily more impersonal as its mobility grows....

"In the dictionaries, solitude and loneliness are the same thing; in life they are not. Obviously, everyone needs some time to hear himself think. Some people are natural solitaries, content with their own company; or, if they believe they have one, with that of their God. Writers, painters, composers, require more solitude than most; heavy responsibility must to some extent set a man apart.

"But loneliness is not a chosen form of isolation. It is a sense of deprivation: the emptiness of the human being who longs for contact with others but who is, through circumstance or temperament, denied it. Solitude is an interval in living, but loneliness is a kind of death."[65]

I suspected that much of this was still relevant in 2004, although the lonely may be less visible now, spending their idle hours in front of television sets, themselves out of view. They represent a pastoral opportunity for pastoral ministry today. The liturgy, with good music and excellent preaching, can summon people out of their isolation and bring them together in community. This is, of course, a religious need but, upon examination, it can also be seen as a pressing social need that can be met through pastoral ministry. And the closer one gets to this problem, I said, the clearer it becomes that many of those most in need are not the elderly, but young men and women who will be open to creative initiatives Jesuits and their lay associates might take in their direction.

It was more than interesting to me to hear, at the end of this two-day conference, an announcement by the Provincial that the British Province would pay special attention to the eighteen- to thirty-six-year-old population as it focused its mission and shaped its ministries for the next half century.

I'm assuming that they've made good progress along those lines. I'm convinced that this is the direction in which enlightened pastoral leadership will be leading the Church in the United States as we move toward the year 2050. My conviction rests on the belief that the Holy Spirit is alive and well in the Church today. The pontificate of Pope Francis is evidence of this. He embodies so much of what this book would regard as essential for effective pastoral leadership.

CHAPTER Eight

Facing Up to the Clergy Sex Abuse Scandal

The elephant in the room whenever pastoral leadership is discussed in contemporary Catholic circles is still the scandal that rocked the American Church in 2002. The Boston Globe broke the story and a film about the Globe's work in doing so—*Spotlight*—won an Academy Award more than a decade later, in 2016. That has helped to open the question up a bit, but we still don't give it the thought that it deserves.

I was pastor at Holy Trinity in Washington, D.C., when that story broke. It seemed both natural and important to me to exercise pastoral leadership by calling a meeting in the parish auditorium immediately after our two concurrent 9:00 a.m. Masses the next Sunday morning to permit interested parishioners to ventilate their feelings and raise questions. I remember simply walking onto the stage in front of about 300 parishioners and saying, "OK, it's a jump ball. Who wants to go first? Any question or comment is fair game." We were still at it two hours later, and we convened again on the following Sunday to keep the conversation going.

Many parishes have yet to provide a forum for this kind of discussion; many pastors have simply remained mum. They call it loyalty; I call it failed leadership.

Letting my imagination run back then, I asked aloud, what if Jesus Christ were to appear in our midst to convene a meeting of all American Catholics, and what if he invited them to reflect aloud on the causes of the scandal. What new ideas might emerge? What new remedial initiatives remain to be tried?

All who would gather in this imaginary assembly would be aware that the disclosures of sexual abuse by clergy triggered the crisis. All would acknowledge that the sins, crimes, and psychological disorders of some clergy were only part of the problem. All would agree that mismanagement of these problems by members of the hierarchy and some religious superiors intensified the crisis. The agenda before this gathering would focus on root-cause analysis of

(1) the conditions that permitted sexual abuse of minors by clergy to happen, and (2) why, on the part of Church authorities, the response to reports of abuse was so badly managed. A wounded Church was in need of answers to these questions.

This imaginary assembly I had in mind would be anything but a triumphant rally of the faithful in the presence of their Lord. Instead, it would be a humble gathering of believers, hoping to be led out of their confusion and anger into a promised future. This is the challenge confronting parish leadership today. The people would gather in quiet trust before the Lord who holds their future in his hands. They would look horizontally (to one another) as well as vertically (to Church authorities) for leadership into the unknown.

I can imagine Jesus opening the assembly with the words he used more than twenty centuries ago and which are often seen as pointing to the signs of the times:

> "When you see [a] cloud rising in the west you say immediately that it is going to rain—and so it does; and when you notice that the wind is blowing from the south you say that it is going to be hot—and so it is. You hypocrites! You know how to interpret the appearance of the earth and the sky; why do you not know how to interpret the present time?" (Lk 12:54-56)

That word "hypocrites" would sting its way through the whole assembly, I'm sure, but it would not be all that wide of the mark. Were it not for the hypocrisy of both leaders and followers in the ranks of the clergy, the press would not have had ready targets on which to pounce. It is always newsworthy when ministers of religion contradict by secret actions the high principles they publicly preach. Such hypocrisy is always fair focus for the outside searchlight—for the "Spotlight," if you will—however harsh the glare. The hypocrisy relates to a reality deserving of no protection from publicity or prosecution.

This is not to say that the sin cannot be forgiven, that those who are ill cannot be treated (although some perhaps may never be completely cured), and that the crime cannot be offset by just punishments, even though the effects of crimes on innocent victims may never go away. Hence absolution, medical treatment, and just retribution for perpetrators will always be part of Church efforts to construct defenses for children and walls of integrity for clergy.

Participants in this imaginary assembly might agree that while relatively few are guilty, all who belong to the Church are responsible for coming up with solutions. Root cause analysis is the place to begin. All should be giving their best thought to the challenge of "how to interpret the present time." It's the whole point of the gathering.

If given the chance to speak in this assembly, I would acknowledge that any contribution of mine is inspired by shame, embarrassment, and lingering anger over what I've read and heard about clergy sexual misconduct. I'm also motivated by an ongoing concern for victims, by disappointment with managerial incompetence in the hierarchy, by a loyalty to the institutional Church, by love for the community of believers who are the Church, and by a personal commitment to priesthood.

The path of analysis begins for me at two entry gates: (1) the threshold one crosses when entering seminary and (2) the advancement to ordination.

If I were a bishop or admitting provincial, I would want to know the sexual history of every candidate. I realize that this is extraordinarily intrusive and invasive of the privacy our culture prizes and fights to protect. But no one would be forced to continue or even to participate in this conversation. No one has a right to become a priest. Yet the conversation between the candidate and the admitting authority to a seminary should, I believe, touch on the delicate questions of how one has managed his sexuality, on whether one's sexual identity is adequately known to himself, and whether one feels truly called to and capable of meeting a commitment to celibacy.

If the candidate had ever himself been sexually abused, that fact should be known. It would not of itself be disqualifying, but would open up an honest examination of whether or not the psychological impact of the violation has been dealt with so that the probability of the victim's ever becoming a violator would be judged minimal. Exquisite care would have to be taken to avoid creating (or aggravating) the impression that the young man caused the abuse or is somehow morally responsible for it. Psychological health, like physical health, is critically important for admission to a seminary. Any child victim of abuse must be a psychologically healthy young adult when entering the seminary. I would say that serious doubt on that score should be disqualifying.

Similarly, when it comes time to advance a seminarian to orders, the same kind of sacred conversation should take place. If the commitment to celibacy has proved to be unmanageable, if anything even remotely resembling the criminal behavior that produced the scandals we all now deplore has occurred during the seminary years, the candidate should be denied admission to orders.

As harsh as these policy guidelines may appear when spoken aloud or laid out in cold print, it would be wise for bishops, religious superiors, and seminary rectors to adopt them and to apply them now *retroactively* to those famous "files" that have been turned over to criminal prosecutors all across the country. What if these guidelines had been in place many years ago when the tragic figures now called "cases" sought admission to the seminary or requested advancement to ordination? Could some subsequent abuse have been prevented? Would not an application of these guidelines have protected children?

Another sacred and privileged communication is involved in what we call "confessional practice." I think careful analysis needs to be applied to the use of the Sacrament of Reconciliation by seminarians and priests, as well as to the responsibilities of the priest-confessor who exercises this ministry.

The seal of Confession must never be violated. That's an absolute. In the present context an enormous responsibility for protecting children rests on the shoulders of both penitent and confessor. There have been kind, saintly, "good confessors" known to Catholics of all generations. Many good priests exercise this ministry today with compassion, prudence, and wisdom. But assume for the moment that the worst of priest perpetrators over the past half century "went to Confession," as we used to say, and repeatedly received sacramental forgiveness for their sexual sins.

Did the confessor know that the penitent was a priest or seminarian? Was the sin confessed in a sufficiently unambiguous way so that the confessor could not miss the fact that the party to the sexual sin was a child? Did the possibility of pedophilia occur to the confessor? Were the circumstances sufficiently explained so that the confessor knew it to be a hetero- or homosexual act, with an adult or minor, with another priest or seminarian, with a married or unmarried person, male or female, minor or mature? And if it was clear that the sin confessed related to criminal abuse of a minor, was absolution withheld? Or, if granted, was absolution given with a firm instruction to do what the confessor himself could never do: inform superiors, notify civil authorities, seek therapy, remove oneself from all contact with children, resign?

The U.S. Conference of Catholic Bishops must, I believe, convene a task force of pastoral and moral theologians, canon lawyers, and professional psychologists to examine confessional practice in the light of what can be learned from the scandals. To the best of my knowledge, this has not yet been done. Workshops for seminarians and priests, especially seminary rectors and retreat directors, and for anyone else involved in seminary formation, are needed regarding what questions or actions are permissible or impermissible, required or not required of the "good confessor" in these cases.

Mismanagement of the problem by some bishops and religious superiors would have to be discussed in my imaginary assembly. Anyone offering an opinion would, I hope, preface his or her remarks with an admission that no one is perfect, hindsight is 20/20, and all the facts are not available even now. It is impossible to know the motivation of bishops and religious superiors whose mismanagement is now evident and whose managerial competence, veracity, integrity, and character are now open to question. Some seem not to have known that particular actions were crimes that had to be reported to public authorities, although that ignorance is just about nonexistent now.

Many in positions of authority in the Church have not yet understood or personally assimilated what I would call the three essentials of Church leadership: availability, accountability, and vulnerability. Many pastors and ecclesiastical superiors were and are strangers to transparency. Can this be remedied without open and honest conversation—not harsh judgmental accusation—just frank, candid exchanges between bishops, priests, and laity, as might happen in the presence of the Lord? Of course not. It is time then for me to pull all this out of the realm of imagination and put it on diocesan and even parochial ground. Let bishops and pastors convene the assemblies.

It is obvious that some bishops and religious superiors simply did not know their men—their strengths and weaknesses, their fears and hopes. It is also obvious that the priest-perpetrators were not always open with their superiors; they dissembled, hid, lied, and knowingly violated sacred trusts. Were some bishops and superiors "too busy" with administrative matters (*administrivia*?) to meet their responsibilities as spiritual fathers of the priests and brothers under their jurisdiction? If they were, would a scheduled, annual or semi-annual one-on-one conversation of accountability between subject and superior close such gaps and provide a measure of safety for potential victims in the future?

Were some "hierarchs" caught up in a promotion culture (not unlike a military culture) that focuses on moving higher up, making them so protective of their own reputations that they chose not to let problems become public that would reflect badly on their leadership? So they buried files and destroyed records. Was ambition the poison at the bottom of this well? Did some ambitious ecclesiastical executives permit concern for their own advancement to override or blind them to the safety needs of children? The question, painful as it is, has to be asked. It can be answered only in the hearts of the responsible leaders. That it must be asked points to the need to cultivate during the seminary years a spirituality that will help aspirants to the priesthood manage their career ambitions in a way that incorporates them into the death and resurrection of Jesus. As the opening words of Chapter 6 explained, they are called to be servant leaders, to follow a Christ who came not "to be served, but to serve and to give his life as a ransom for many" (Mt 20:28).

Pope Francis seems to think that the elimination of honorary titles like "Monsignor" might help to reduce competitive pressures—i.e., pressures to compete for advancement. I think he's right.

If bishops and pastors do in fact convene assemblies for discussion of these issues, the question of "places of honor" will surely come up. Any contemporary assembly would, I suspect, exhibit some signs of a flattening out, a de-layering that is most appropriate for a faith community that has experienced an erosion of trust in its hierarchy. It would in no way signal disrespect or diminution of authority, just a humble awareness that priest and bishop are servants; they are there to serve one another and their people. They belong in the center of a circle, not at the top of a pyramid. This means servant leadership and servant followership with no thought or argument as to "who is the greatest" (Mt 18:1).

Returning for a moment to my imaginary assembly, suppose there was a question-and-answer exchange in which Jesus were to call upon one of our cardinals. Would Jesus address him as "Your Eminence" or call him by his first name? Is it unimaginable that both laity and clergy might come to address their bishops and cardinals by their baptismal names—not nicknames or titles of familiarity—but formal first names? Not likely in our time, but who can say?

The late Cardinal Joseph Bernardin, in his first meeting with his priests in the cathedral shortly after arriving in Chicago, borrowed a line from Scripture to introduce himself, "I am Joseph, your brother" (Gn 45:4). Formal first-name address would be a modest but far-reaching change bringing leader and led closer together in mutual respect. Or perhaps an easier-to-implement change would be to take a page from the military book and address higher-ups by the rank they hold. "Cardinal," "Archbishop," and "Bishop" would be just fine and might breed new respect there on the humble ruins of fallen "eminences" and extinguished "excellencies" in our wounded American Church.

Future candidates for the episcopacy might be wiser, better choices if their candidacy were announced publicly months in advance in the diocese from which they entered the seminary, the diocese in which they currently serve, and the diocese to which they are being proposed for service. This suggestion recalls the "banns of marriage" once routinely read in parish churches, allowing anyone who believes with good reason that the marriage should not take place to come forward. Knowing that past misdeeds might be raised publicly as objections to his elevation to the rank of bishop, or, if he is already a bishop being proposed for transfer from one diocese to another, a man with sexual misconduct in his past would have to be uncommonly ambitious to run the risk. Once the nominations were made public, anyone with facts supporting questions about the appropriateness of the appointment could make them known in confidence to the office of the papal nuncio in Washington, D.C.

Another change (which, had it been in place, might have discouraged some bishops from shuttling priest offenders from parish to parish) would be having a few members of the parish council appointed to a review committee that would function as credentialing committees do in most hospitals. No physician is appointed to the staff without a review of credentials, competence, and both professional and personal behavior. Members of a parish have a right to know, at least through a confidential review by their elected lay representatives, the "record" of any priest about to be assigned to serve them. Honesty would require full disclosure on the part of a bishop or provincial of any "problems" in the personnel file of the man being proposed for assignment. This, of course, presumes the integrity and completeness of the file in the first place.

If bishops and pastors do convene assemblies, lay participants will surely ask why local or diocesan pastoral councils are not more effective, suggesting, if canonically permissible, the introduction of a "separation of powers" in every diocese so that the bishop alone is not the legislative, executive, and judicial "tree" in our one-branch (corporation sole) diocesan Church government. Realizing that the Church is not a democracy, lay observers might suggest that regional tribunals be set up to handle canonical trials of offending clergy. This would be a change that would prevent any single bishop from acting independently of the other bishops in his region. Episcopal authority that is unaccountable to anyone "below" and neither evaluated by nor subject to judgment by episcopal peers, is authority easily abused (and when abused, difficult to correct).

If given the opportunity, many lay voices are likely to remind the clergy that the Church is a "family-owned business." Family members have a right to be kept informed of how the business is doing; this means public audits of finances based on uniform accounting systems in all "branches"—i.e., every diocese, every parish!

Some are likely to insist that management institutes for all bishops be mandatory; the "curriculum" would involve case studies and "best practices" recommendations. Orientation programs for not-yet-installed bishops could, like the advanced management programs offered by top business schools for rising executives, protect new bishops from making the serious mistakes that have come to light during the clergy sex abuse scandal.

Organizational change never happens suddenly, yet some adjustments are happening all the time. Enlightened criticism can bring about structural adjustments that will eventually lead to significant change.

John W. Gardner, who, from 1965 until 1968 served as U.S. Secretary of Health, Education, and Welfare, was a wise observer of the human condition. In a 1968 commencement address at Cornell University, he noted that historians would look back at the social turmoil of that period and see that institutions of higher education then "were caught in a savage crossfire between unloving critics and uncritical lovers."[66] The uncritical lovers wanted "to smother their institutions in the embrace of death, loving their rigidities more than their promise, shielding them from life-giving criticism."[67] The unloving critics wanted to tear the institutions apart; they were "skilled in demolition but untutored in the arts by which human institutions are nurtured and strengthened and made to flourish."[68]

Criticism without cool reason will not help the Church today. True, the Church is not a human institution, but it must be obedient to the laws of growth and sensitive to the way institutions change. All who participate in the assemblies I've suggested will have to check the impulse to substitute blame for analysis and, aware that grace builds upon nature, do all that is naturally possible to strengthen the institutional Church.

Root cause analysis will, by definition, lead to the roots of the current problem. The analytical lines that I have traced here suggest the need for: (1) more fully informed seminary admission standards; (2) tighter criteria for advancement to orders; (3) a spirituality of priesthood informed by humility and a commitment to celibacy; (4) an examination of confessional practice; (5) reduction, if not elimination, of honorific titles and places of honor in the ecclesiastical culture; (6) an annual "accountability conversation" between diocesan priest and bishop; (7) a credential review and quality assessment role for laity in selection of parish clergy; (8) advance public announcement of the names of all being considered for service as bishop; and (9) management training that imparts "best practice" skills while emphasizing "availability, accountability, and vulnerability" as essential qualifications for work as a bishop.

Complacency will kill the search for root causes. Enlightened leadership at the pastoral level must never permit that to happen

CHAPTER Nine

The Shepherd Leader

Chapter 6 dealt with "Servant Leadership," a congenial term for leadership in our Church and an appropriate ideal for all who minister in the Church, especially for pastors, bishops, cardinals, and the Holy Father. And Chapter 8 documented how the past 15 years or so have brought difficult days for both leadership and followership in the Catholic Church. They've also been difficult days for leaders in the business community, in education, in government and in international affairs. Leaders in any area of life must display, as I've already indicated, three characteristics; they must be available, accountable, and vulnerable.

Our faith tradition has another image of leadership with which I want to close out this overview of parish leadership, namely, the Good Shepherd, who, as you know from Scripture (Jn 10:11), is prepared to give his life for his sheep. Let's call this "shepherd leadership" and use it as a category to encapsulate the best that we hope for in renewed parish leadership.

The shepherd leader is there for and with the followership: "the sheep hear his voice" (Jn 10:3). The shepherd leader knows his own: The shepherd "calls his own sheep by name" (Jn 10:3), and "[H]e walks ahead of them, and the sheep follow him, because they recognize his voice" (Jn 10:4).

You get a fuller picture of the Good Shepherd if you read the surrounding verses to the several that I have quoted here from the tenth chapter of the Gospel of John. Read the entire tenth chapter of John's Gospel and you'll see what I mean. For example, in John 10:7, Jesus compares himself to the gate of the sheepfold. "I am the gate for the sheep. Whoever enters through me will be saved, and will come in and go out and find pasture." And in John 10:10, "I came that they might have life and have it more abundantly." That is what shepherd leaders are called to do—to enable their followers to live fuller lives, to have life and have it more abundantly.

In the present crisis of leadership confronting the Catholic Church in the United States, a helpful lesson might be learned from two contemporary business writers. Note that they are writing about business leaders. One way to stop a business leader in his or her tracks, write consultants Robert Goffee and Gareth Jones, is to ask: "Why Should Anyone Be Led by You?" That question is the title of an article these observers wrote for the *Harvard Business Review*. "Without fail," say the authors, "the response is a sudden, stunned hush. All you can hear are knees knocking."[69]

The question is a good one to put to anyone in a leadership position anywhere. How would a cardinal, bishop, or pastor respond to that question today? The reply has to be something more substantial than, "I've been assigned." Leadership implies voluntary followership. If you're the leader, why should anybody follow?

Goffee and Jones give a backward glance through history and acknowledge that there have been widely accepted leadership traits and styles. But they change over time. Today, these authors argue, the times require that "Leaders should let their weaknesses be known. By exposing a measure of vulnerability, they make themselves approachable and show themselves to be human." Today's leaders, say these authors, have to adapt to "endless contingencies" while making decisions suited to a particular situation. They have to be "good situation sensors [able to] collect and interpret soft data."

Why should knees knock when a leader is asked, "Why should anyone be led by you?" If the so-called leader has specialized in unavailability, unaccountability, and presumed invulnerability, the question could be quite discomfiting. Those in leadership positions in our Church today should be wise enough to ask themselves why they are there, and the answer cannot be anything but to serve. And those who constitute the followership—that would include all parishioners— can exercise their own quiet leadership by raising that question ever so gently whenever circumstances warrant it. Circumstances in our Church do indeed warrant it today. Good, faithful Catholics are asking hard but helpful questions that will help us work our way through the present crisis.

We all acknowledge that authority and leadership are not the same thing. The authority conferred by sacrament and ecclesiastical system on pastor, bishop, or pope is not now being questioned. The question is whether or not the person in authority possesses the ability to lead.

Shepherd leaders are up front and open. Transparency is not a threat to them. Service and sacrifice are their very reason for existence.

It was striking to me to read in the business press more than a decade ago that Joseph Berardino, the chairman of the accounting firm Arthur Andersen, stepped down in the hope that his resignation could save his staff and their company. "Andersen Chief Says He Quit as a Sacrifice to Aid the Staff," the headline read in the *New York Times* on March 28, 2002. And that, of course, related to the problems this accounting firm faced as a result of its failure to conduct an adequate audit of the Enron Corporation. Shepherd leaders are no strangers to sacrifice, but it was striking to find the term "sacrifice" in the business press, not in the religious press reporting on the clergy sex abuse crisis.

What we have been reflecting on in this book illustrates the need in the Church for Good Shepherd leadership. It is needed in parishes of all sizes in all places, seasons, and circumstances. To the extent that we are all leaders, there is something here for each one of us to apply to ourselves, to ponder over, to pray about. What kind of leader are you to those who follow you in family, classroom, store, shop, office, parish, or organization of any kind?

And there is something here for us to keep in mind as we ponder and pray for our cardinals, bishops, pastors and other Church leaders in their effort to become not just good, but better shepherds. The Church is us—all of us. The Church is the people of God. The Church is you and I. It is saint and sinner. The Church includes the offender and the victim. The Church is more than the pope, the cardinals, bishops, priests and religious around the world. The Church is all the laity together with their religious and priests, bishops, cardinals, and the Holy Father.

We are the Church. We are a Church in crisis, and we have been for well over a decade. We are all in this together. We all have to respond. Consider your response to this crisis in the spirit and style of the Good Shepherd. Consider what you might do by way of prayer and fasting. Consider how you might lead, how you might be a shepherd leader, by exercising responsible followership in grateful fidelity to the Christ who called you and suffered for you, leaving you an example that you should follow in his footsteps. Follow you will. Lead you must. And never forget that Jesus, the good and eternal shepherd, said to you, to me, to us who are the Church, "I came so that they might have life and have it more abundantly" (Jn 10:10).

CHAPTER Ten

Change Is at the Heart of Leadership

In 1973, I became Dean of Arts and Sciences at Loyola University in New Orleans. Loyola is separated from Tulane University by a property line; the two campuses are contiguous. In those days (it may still be the case; I just don't know), there was a modest amount of cross-registration and informal cooperation between the two institutions. So, since I was new to higher education administration, and the Tulane dean, Joe Cronin, had been on the job for eighteen years, I thought it would be not just courteous, but wise, for me to walk over and get acquainted with my counterpart.

It was a pleasant meeting. In what some might regard as a sudden burst of humility on my part, I asked the Tulane dean if he had any advice to offer to help me get off to a good start. "You will soon learn," said this veteran academic administrator, "that it is easier to move a cemetery than to move a liberal arts faculty."

How right he was!

Most people resist change and prefer to live in the immediate past. Psychologists might nuance that observation by saying that it is loss, not change, that people fear. What they have, they know. The familiar is, by definition, in hand; it is a possession. To let go amounts to a loss. Rarely do they regard it as good riddance; more often than not, they see it as loss. Since leaders are in the business of bringing about change, they have to be sensitive to the perception of loss on the part of those whom they are trying to lead.

James J. Schiro, chairman of Zurich Financial Services is quoted in the "Corner Office" feature of the Sunday business section of the *New York Times* as saying, "People don't like change, but they can manage change. They can't handle uncertainty. I think it is the job of leaders to eliminate uncertainty."[70] We live in an uncertain world, but that does not condemn us to a state of hesitation and indecision. Uncertainty, like change, can be managed. Obstacles can be overcome. Decisions can be made—indeed, *must* be made—if progress is going to be achieved.

Leadership is about getting people to tackle tough problems. That is the view of Ronald Heifetz, whose work has been nicely summarized by Sharon Daloz Parks in *Leadership Can Be Taught: A Bold Approach for a Complex World* (Boston: Harvard Business School Press, 2005), a book, by the way, that could be a great gift to any priest pastor. Tough problems abound not only in higher education but in virtually every corner of organizational life where leadership operates, including parishes. Just ask any leader, including your pastor!

Art Hauptman is a veteran observer of change in higher education. (It is interesting to note, by the way, that *Change* is the name of a fine magazine that has been serving the higher education community in the U.S. since the 1960s.) Mr. Hauptman has written wisely and often about strategic change in higher education. On one such occasion he defined a "strategic response" as "a decision controlled by institutional officials that (1) requires changing a major policy, program, or practice and (2) involves some risk."

Note first that when it comes to bringing about change, institutional officials (management and trustees) have control; next, something "major" is at stake, and third, a certain degree of risk is involved. The risk is inescapable, as is the responsibility on the part of "officials" to bring about the change.

Just as strategic planning should go before any major change, strategic thinking should precede the plan. Strategic thinking begins with the question: What sets us apart? That's another way of asking about "comparative advantage." Your comparative advantage could be nothing more than your location and your people; they are uniquely yours and they set you apart from the rest of the pack. What to do with what is uniquely yours is for leaders (and here I'm including pastors) to decide, but not without consulting others. Such decisions will almost always involve change. I say "almost" because there will be times when the leader has to resist change, stand fast in the face of opposition, even stand down if principle requires it. But that would be the exception, not the rule. Leadership is indeed about change, even though it might not be all about change.

Thinking strategically is second nature to the experienced leader. And, as Tom Ricks has observed, strategy "is a grand-sounding word" that

> is frequently misused by laymen as a synonym for tactics. In fact, strategy has a very different and quite simple meaning that flows from just one short set of questions: Who are we, and what are we ultimately trying to do here? How will we do it, and what resources and means will we employ in doing it? The four answers give rise to one's strategy. Ideally, one's tactics will then follow from them—that is, this is who we are, this is the outcome we wish to achieve, this is how we aim to do it, and this is what we will use to do it.[71]

Knowing who you are ("this is who we are"); knowing your immediate goal ("this is the outcome we wish to achieve"); knowing how you are going to get there ("this is how we aim to do it"); and identifying the resources you will need ("this is what we will use to do it")—all this begins with strategy and ends with tactics. Leaders bring strategy, which is the product of vision, into partnership with tactics, which are the immediate objectives. Strategy is a long-run consideration; tactics are short-term steps. Working together they produce progress. Only by working together can they overcome resistance to change.

Change involves process. It takes time. It presupposes vision, of course, and requires clear and persistent communication. To say that change takes time is another way of saying that it requires patience in the persons who initiate, manage, and are affected by the process.

The best book I've encountered on the relationship of change to leadership is titled *Leading Change* by John P. Kotter.[72] It is organized around an eight-stage change process. Each stage involves a leadership responsibility. I will first describe the eight stages noting that these are relevant to parishes, not just to businesses.

The initial stage is establishing a sense of urgency. Next, the leader has to form a "guiding coalition," a group with enough power to lead the change. Third, there must be the identification of a vision to propel the effort, accompanied by strategies for achieving the vision. Communication comes next; it is in this fourth stage that a seemingly endless repetition, by word and example, of the vision and strategies begins. Stage five is what construction workers would call "clearing and grubbing"—getting rid of obstacles, eliminating whatever would undermine the change vision. Sixth, there should be periodic pauses to celebrate the "wins" along the way, not to declare victory or encourage complacency, just to recognize and reward where recognition might be due. The seventh stage can be a "decade-long process" that consolidates the gains while avoiding triumphalism and facilitating still more change. Finally, the new ways of doing things must be "anchored" in the culture. Let's examine that process, stage by stage.

URGENCY. This is not a call for a pressure-cooker work environment, or running an assembly line through the executive suite, or adopting a metrics-driven performance schedule. It is an on-your-toes, heads-up, wide-awake posture that amounts to an organizational refusal to become complacent. You don't have to be ill in order to get better. So why presume, when you are healthy and things are going very well, that they couldn't be going better? And since "going better" means better for all—clients, customers, workplace associates, shareholders, and all other stakeholders, including the community within which you operate—how can you not want to see that happen? Once a decision for change has been made, a sense of urgency must accompany it all the way through every stage of implementation.

GUIDING COALITION. Recall the center-of-the-circle location, as opposed to the top-of-the- pyramid imagery that I mentioned earlier. Think now of a sawed-off pyramid and notice that there is plenty of room there, on a platform near the top, for a leadership team, what John Kotter, whose eight stages we are reviewing here, would call a "guiding coalition." Leadership is indeed all about change. That change must be guided by a leadership coalition, a group that has the power to lead the change. We're not talking here about a king and his court, a ruler with a few advisers. This is a team of leaders who trust one another, share a vision, and have sufficient authority to make things happen.

Kotter lists "four key characteristics" as essential if the guiding coalition is to be effective: (1) "position power"—all key positions in the organization are included, no one capable of blocking progress is left out; (2) "expertise"—the required competencies needed to get the job done are represented; (3) "credibility"—all members of the team have good reputations and are respected throughout the organization; (4) "leadership"—the group has "enough proven leaders to be able to drive the change process."[73] Kotter adds: "Two types of individuals should be avoided at all costs when putting together a guiding coalition. The first have egos that fill up a room, leaving no space for anybody else. The second are what I call snakes, people who create enough mistrust to kill teamwork."[74]

What do you do if these two types occupy some of those key positions that have to be part of the coalition? You've got a major problem that has to be solved by transfer or termination before the process of change can begin. This is one of the toughest challenges leaders have to face. Failure to meet this challenge is the reason so much hoped-for change never happens. This, however, is a less likely to be the case in a parish than in a large, complex business organization.

VISION. "Without a vision, the people perish," says the Book of Proverbs (Pv 29:18). The wisdom of that ancient assertion is indisputable. The question then becomes: Where does the vision originate, and how is it translated into a plan for change? It originates in the mind of the leader or the collective mind of the leadership group. It won't emerge unless there is imagination at work between the ears of those who would lead. They then have to reduce the vision to strategy on the way to fashioning a strategic plan.

Individuals throughout the organization will rally around a clear vision, presuming of course, that it is also the right vision (ethically and strategically correct). The right vision will unify and motivate the people. And remember that without a vision, the people will wander off into purposeless make-work activity; eventually they, or more accurately, their organization, will perish. If the vision is really clear, down-the-line managers and individual associates can figure out for themselves what needs doing in a given situation.

Effective visions, says Kotter, will be imaginable, desirable, feasible, focused, flexible, and communicable.

COMMUNICATION. John Kotter's propensity to produce numbered stages and lists of principles works well for his readers on this important point. There are seven principles that he offers to facilitate effective communication of a vision: (1) Keep it simple. (2) Use metaphors, analogies, examples. (3) Use many different forums. (4) Repeat, repeat, repeat. (5) Walk the talk, or lead by example. (6) Explicitly address seeming inconsistencies. (7) Listen and be listened to.

ELIMINATING THE OBSTACLES. This stage of the change process relates to the "empowerment" of people throughout the organization. The "barriers to empowerment," as Kotter sees them, are the realities in any given organization that tend to box people in. There are (1) structural barriers, (2) a lack of the needed skills, (3) inadequate information systems, and (4) "troublesome supervisors"— people who refuse to get with the program but possess enough power to slow it down, even sabotage it.

How do you deal with the particularly "difficult person" who is clearly blocking progress? Kotter is good on this point and remember that it is as applicable in a parish as it is in a complex business organization:

> From what I've seen, the best solution to this kind of problem is usually honest dialogue. Here's the story with the industry, the company, our vision, the assistance we need from you, and the time frame in which we need all this. What can we do to help you help us? If the situation really is hopeless, and the person needs to be replaced, that fact often becomes clear early in this dialogue. If the person wants to help but feels blocked, the discussion can identify solutions. If the person wants to help but is incapable of doing so, the clearer expectations and timetable can eventually make his or her removal less contentious. The basic fairness of this approach helps overcome guilt. The rational and thoughtful dialogue also helps minimize the risk that good short-term results will suddenly turn bad or that [the dissenter] will be able to launch a successful political counterattack.[75]

It would be all so easy if we lived in a friction-free world with no ill will, incompetence, mean-spiritedness, and no unreasonable demands. But we don't and never will. So relational skills, patience, persuasion, and a fair measure of luck will always be needed to keep the change process moving forward.

SHORT-TERM WINS. Failure to celebrate small wins along the way represents lost opportunities to recharge the batteries that fuel the progress. Moreover, failure to celebrate is risky. You risk losing momentum. But when you do give recognition to short-term wins, you also run the risk of letting the celebration get out of hand, producing a complacency capable of impeding further progress. The point of giving public recognition and modest rewards is to shore up what might otherwise become sagging spirits, thus keeping all shoulders firmly fixed to the wheel and all eyes focused on the distance not yet covered. Instead of tooting your horn at a decibel level that registers as hyperbole, try the quiet background music of encouragement as accompaniment to continuing progress.

"The primary purpose of the first six phases of the transformation process is to build up sufficient momentum to blast through the dysfunctional granite walls found in so many organizations. When we ignore any of these steps, we put all our efforts at risk."[76] Dysfunctional granite wall? Count your blessings if you haven't encountered them; recommit yourself to an understanding of leadership as "the art of inducing others to follow" is you want to get around them.

CONSOLIDATING GAINS. Recognizing that change takes time and that many glitches can stall the process, leadership has to view what has been achieved thus far as if it were a ball of consolidated gains that must keep rolling. It won't roll unless "the guiding coalition uses the credibility afforded by short-term wins to tackle additional and bigger change projects."[77] It won't roll unless "additional people are brought in, promoted, and developed to help with all the changes;"[78] unless "senior people focus on maintaining clarity of shared purpose for the overall effort and keeping urgency levels up;"[79] unless "lower ranks in the hierarchy both provide leadership for specific projects and manage those projects;"[80] and unless "unnecessary interdependencies"[81] are eliminated. Interdependencies are those permission points and reporting centers that have a way of multiplying in organizational life. Keep them to a necessary minimum; otherwise the quicksand effect will soon be felt.

ANCHORING. The final stage of the change process involves "anchoring" the change—the new way of doing things—in the organization's culture. A culture, as I explained earlier, is a set of shared meanings and values. Everyone buys in. The values are shared. Their meaning is clear. Cultures are defined by dominant values. Cultures influence behavior. So, for all practical purposes, nothing will have changed unless the change is anchored in the culture.

Not So Fast.

Most of what I have presented so far in this chapter comes from Boston, from the Harvard Business School; it is the work of John Kotter, whose book is published by the Harvard Business School Press. A qualifying perspective, not contradictory, just qualifying, comes from Palo Alto, from Stanford Business Books in the form of a study titled *Change the Way You Lead Change*, with the not-so-modest subtitle *Leadership Strategies that REALLY Work*.[82] What's going on here? The authors, David Herold and Donald Fedor, have their academic home in the College of Management at Georgia Tech. Their book states that:

> the majority of other books, articles, and seminars on organizational change [like Kotter's] focus their attention addressing HOW to implement change, that is, the change process. The recommended process 'dos' and 'don'ts' of change implementation are the result of many years of practitioner and research observations about things that tend, in general, to help or hinder change implementation.... For example, we've all heard about the need for a change vision; the importance of communication; the need to motivate people to change by means of creating a 'burning platform'; and the importance of involving others, celebrating victories, and reinforcing the appropriate behaviors. These recommendations are based on a great deal of evidence that if leaders do not effectively communicate, motivate, involve, or reinforce, the results of change efforts will often be disappointing. Surely, if leaders all followed these prescriptions, most changes would turn out well. But they don't. Why?"[83]

Herold and Fedor find that "change is never a straightforward, stepwise, linear, or easily prescribed process. Rather, it is messy and complicated, and its outcomes are easily swayed by a host of factors, making prediction of success difficult at best."[84] The root causes of the failed change efforts their research analyzed were not related to problems with the change process. "Rather, they were often systemic or situational factors that doomed the planned changes no matter how much attention was paid to process."[85] In addition:

> [W]hile some disappointing change efforts could be diagnosed as suffering from "communication," "vision," or "sense of urgency" issues, more often than not, the lists of most recommended change steps did not map onto leaders' lists of root causes for failed changes. These recommendations could not explain failures due to pursuit of bad change ideas; failures due to the inadequacy of those asked to lead change; failures attributable to the behaviors of those expected to implement the changes; failures attributable to cultural and intraorganizational factors; or failures attributable to factors in the organization's environment.[86]

They are saying, in effect, that the proposed change isn't going to happen if it is not, first and foremost, a good idea. Nor will it happen if it is not in the hands of able leaders. Moreover, there are cultural and environmental considerations outside the organization that could prevent an otherwise good change-idea from surviving long enough to become a viable program or project, a really new way of doing things that becomes rooted in the organization's culture.

There are no guarantees. Even the best leaders are not immune to bad luck. Those who address the challenge of change (as all leaders must) would do well to carry an adequate supply of what is called "humbition," a practical blend of humility and ambition.

In more technical language, Herold and Fedor put it this way: "Slowly, we came to understand that successful changes require leaders to develop better ways of analyzing (1) *what* they think they want or need to change, (2) what they know about *themselves* and the *others* who will be asked to lead and make the behavioral adjustments implied by the change, and (3) what they know about the *context* in which the change is to occur, especially about what other changes are taking place. Only then can change leaders develop a strategy for *how* they will go about it, when they will do what, and how fast they can move."[87]

If you can pull this off, you are a "savvy change leader" in the estimation of the co-authors of *Change the Way You Lead Change*. Their book will introduce you to famous examples of the savvy and not-so-savvy, who either established themselves at the top or fell from the ranks of corporate leadership in recent years.

PULLING UP THE ANCHOR

The importance of "anchoring" a change in the corporate culture was mentioned above, but you cannot assume that subsequent change will never be necessary. When and if it is, how do you go about lifting the anchor to allow for new and necessary change? *McKinsey Quarterly*, the online journal of McKinsey & Co., addressed this question in a 2009 article titled, "The Crisis: Mobilizing Boards for Change." The board must become involved; but how? Those who chair the boards must lead the way. Read "parish council" for "board" in what follows.

The phenomenon of "anchoring" leads to anchored thinking. Board procedures become anchored also. There are fixed patterns to meetings, agendas, and even to the time allocated for discussion of policy matters on the meeting agenda. An annual off-site meeting that encourages free-wheeling discussion is not a solution, if that meeting won't happen for another six or nine months. The rhythm of the normal monthly or quarterly board meeting has to be disturbed; otherwise, anchored thinking will rule the organizational roost. What to do?

The solution is to explicitly change the way the board interacts. The chairman should insist that members articulate what they have thought but have not had the confidence to express. These conversations will often be more conceptual than rote, and participants will have to take the risk of "saying something stupid." Chairmen will need to muster up the courage to drive relentlessly the discussions that will take most boards into deep and frightening waters. Long-cherished assumptions, existing plans, or defined ambitions may go down the drain.[88]

McKinsey recommends the Edward de Bono "six thinking hats" technique to force board members into new conversations. Each "hat" represents a different way of approaching a problem. Visit www.debono-consulting.com, and you will learn that white-hat thinking focuses on data, facts, and known or needed information; black-hat thinking centers on difficulties and potential problems; red-hat thinking focuses on feelings, hunches, and intuition; green-hat thinking features creativity—possibilities, new ideas; yellow-hat thinking centers on values and benefits; and blue-hat thinking deals with forcing the thinking process to include next steps and action plans.

Members of the board have to say which hat they are wearing. As the discussion proceeds, the chair or facilitator has to keep an eye on those hats that are being over- or underused. This is a leadership role for board chairs. In effect, they are pulling up the anchor and preparing the way for still another change process to begin.

THE WEATHER OUTSIDE

Throughout this chapter, the emphasis has fallen on change within an organization and the virtual certainty that there will be resistance from within. Not to be overlooked, of course, is resistance from without—the expected opposition that new initiatives (typically expansionary) will trigger once word gets out that an institution is on the grow. I can still hear an angry neighborhood community activist at an open meeting in the late 1960s shouting at an official of the mammoth Johns Hopkins Medical Center in East Baltimore, "Fix your boundaries; set your perimeter! No more expansion into our neighborhood! We won't let you do it!'"

That was an exercise of leadership on the part of the activist and a test of leadership for the Hopkins official. Those exchanges continue to happen all the time. Take Fordham University in New York for example. Their main campus is an oasis in the Bronx; they also have a compact Lincoln Center campus in midtown Manhattan. *The New York Times* reported in 2009 that Fordham wanted to expand at Lincoln Center:

> For more than a decade, Fordham University officials have been trying to figure out how to address overcrowding at their Manhattan campus and fill the coffers of their relatively small endowment. They thought the answers to both could be found in one of their most valuable assets: their Manhattan real estate.
>
> So for four years, Fordham officials have been trying to win support from community groups and city officials for plans to turn their four-building site into a far denser 12-building campus in the same space between Amsterdam and Columbus Avenues and 60th and 62nd Streets. Fordham uses the site for various graduate programs ....
>
> The completed campus next to Lincoln Center would have three million square feet of classrooms, libraries and dormitories. It would also include two lots that Fordham would sell to luxury apartment developers, using the profits to bolster the endowment.
>
> After going back and forth with the Department of City Planning on its proposal, the school received permission on Nov. 17 to move ahead and seek approval from various government agencies. The university has begun the uniform land-use review procedure, which includes

public hearings and votes by several layers of public officials. It hopes to start construction later this year, saying the project could take 25 years to complete.

But Fordham has already suffered a setback: At a raucous meeting on Wednesday night, Community Board 7 rejected the plan 31 to 0. The meeting was punctuated by shouts of disapproval from more than 150 neighbors, many of whom waved signs with slogans like "No to the Fordham Fortress."[89]

What's a Fordham leader to do? That, of course, is the question that confronted Fordham's president and his leadership team. The Board 7 vote was just advisory. It didn't stop the proposal from moving up the line. But the overwhelming opposition seemed daunting. The City Councilwoman who represents the neighborhood called for changes in the plan. "'We like Fordham,' she said, 'but the project is too big. We'll keep talking.'"

The talk did continue. Fordham prevailed.

Parish leadership will not have to deal with real estate issues that match the scale of the problem Fordham had to confront. But parish leadership will have to deal with change and the examples discussed in this chapter—especially the necessity of forming a coalition for change—will help parish leadership understand how positive change happens.

The Catholic Church in the United States today stands in need of revitalization and positive change. That is just another way of saying it stands in need of pastoral leadership. By the will of the Father and the work of the Holy Spirit, that will happen on God's own timetable and in God's own way.

When I served as pastor of Holy Trinity in Georgetown, we had a large-letter inscription just above the rear exit of the church. The inscription was there to encourage people to read it as they left church to return to their weekday lives and workweek responsibilities where they might also contribute to the social justice agenda of their church. Here are those words. I invite you to take them along as you leave this book behind:

> "Lord, when did we see you hungry and feed you, or thirsty and give you drink? When did we see you a stranger and welcome you, or naked and clothe you? When did we see you ill or in prison, and visit you?" And the king will say to them in reply: "Amen, I say to you, whatever you did for one of these least brothers [or sisters] of mine, you did for me." (Mt 25:37–40)

Enlightened parish leadership can make this happen.

About the Author

Jesuit Father William J. Byron is University Professor of Business and Society at St. Joseph's University, Philadelphia, PA. He is past president of the University of Scranton (1975–82), The Catholic University of America (1982–92), Loyola University of New Orleans (2003–04), and served as interim president of St. Joseph's Preparatory School in Philadelphia in 2006-2008. He was director of Georgetown University's Center for the Advanced Study of Ethics (1994–97) and taught courses on the social responsibilities of business in the McDonough School of Business at Georgetown. He was pastor of Holy Trinity Catholic Church in Georgetown from 2000 to 2003 and now engages in weekend parish ministry in suburban Philadelphia.

Born in 1927, Fr. Byron received his early parochial school education in Philadelphia, graduated from St. Joseph's Preparatory School, served as an army paratrooper at the end of World War II, attended St. Joseph's College (now University) on the G.I. Bill of Rights, joined the Jesuits in 1950, studied philosophy and economics at St. Louis University, received advance degrees in theology at Woodstock College in Maryland, where he was ordained to the priesthood in 1961, and later earned a doctorate in economics at the University of Maryland. He is the author of twenty books and editor of two, and the recipient of thirty honorary degrees. He writes a bi-weekly general interest column called "Looking Around" for the Catholic News Service Syndicate.

CHAPTER **Notes**

1. Christopher Fry, *A Sleep of Prisoners* (New York: Dramatists Play Service, 1953), p. 62. Spelling of the word enterprise has been altered from the author's original.

2. James Agee, "The Bomb," *Time*, August 20, 1945 in James Agee, *Selected Journalism*, ed. Paul Ashdown (Knoxville: University of Tennessee Press, 2005).

3. Agee, pp. 160–161.

4. Agee, pp. 160–161.

5. Martin Luther King, Jr., as quoted in Michael Hansbury, *The Quality of Leadership* (New Delhi: Epitome Books, 2009), p. 75.

6. John Henry Newman, *Meditations and Devotions of the Late Cardinal Newman* (New York: Longmans, Green, and Co., 1903), pp. 301-302. Spelling of the word *connection* has been altered from the author's original.

7. Robert Frost, "Snow" in *The Poetry of Robert Frost: The Collected Poems*, ed. Edward Connery Lathem (New York: Henry Holt and Company, 1979), pp. 147–148.

8. *Sharing Catholic Social Teaching: Challenges and Directions* (Washington, D.C.: United States Catholic Conference, 1998), p. 1.

9. Shusaku Endo, *Silence*, trans. William Johnston (New York: Taplinger, 1980), p. 86.

10. Pius XI, Encyclical on Reconstruction of the Social Order *Quadragesimo anno* (May 15, 1931), 135.Vatican website. http://www.vatican.va.

11. Paul VI, Declaration on Religious Freedom *Dignitatis humanae* (December 7, 1965), 9, in *Vatican Council II, Volume 1: The Conciliar and Post Conciliar Documents*, ed. Austin Flannery, O.P. (New York: Costello, 1998), p. 806.

12. Associated Press, "Stem Cell Research Foes Losing Clout," *The Boston Globe*, November 24, 2008, /http://archive.boston.com/news/nation/washington/articles/2008/11/24/stem_cell_research_foes_losing_clout/.

13. Joseph Cardinal Bernardin, *Selected Works of Joseph Cardinal Bernardin, Volume 2*, ed. Alphonse P. Spilly, C.PP.S. (Collegeville, Minn.: The Liturgical Press, 2000), p. 82.

14. Bernardin, p. 108.

15. John Courtney Murray, S.J., *We Hold These Truths: Catholic Reflections on the American Proposition* (Lanham, Md.: Rowman & Littlefield, 2005), p. 24.

16. Paul VI, Encyclical on the Development of Peoples *Populorum progressio* (March 26, 1967), 43 (Washington, D.C.: USCC, 1967).

17. John XXIII, Encyclical on Christianity and Social Progress, *Mater et magistra* (May 15, 1961), 59. (Glen Rock, N.J.: Paulist Press, 1961).

18. John XXIII, 59.

19. John Paul II, Apostolic exhortation on the Encounter with the Living Jesus Christ: The Way to Conversion, Communion and Solidarity in America *Ecclesia in America* (January 22, 1999), 69.3. Vatican website: www.vatican.va.

20. Paul VI, Pastoral Constitution on the Church in the Modern World *Gaudium et spes* (December 7, 1965), 27. Vatican website: www.vatican.va.

21. Paul VI, *Populorum progressio*, 47.

22. *Sharing Catholic Social Teaching*, p. 5.

23. *Sharing Catholic Social Teaching*, p. 5.

24. John XXIII, *Mater et magistra*, 91.

25. Abraham Joshua Heschel, *The Insecurity of Freedom: Essays on Human Existence* (New York: Farrar, Straus & Giroux, 1966), p. 93.

26. Francis, Encyclical on Care for Our Common Home *Laudato si'* (May 24, 2015), 3. Vatican website: www.vatican.va.

27. Aristotle, *Politics*, trans. Benjamin Jowett, ed. H.W.C. Davis (New York: Cosimo Classics, 2008), p. 57.

28. Edmund Burke, *The Wisdom of Burke: Extracts from His Speeches and Writings* (London: John Murray, 1886), p. 241.

29. *Sharing Catholic Social Teaching*, p. 4.

30. Joe Hill, "There Is Power in a Union," in Philip Dray, *There Is Power in a Union: The Epic Story of Labor in America*, (New York: Anchor, 2011), p. 350.

31. *Respecting the Just Rights of Workers: Guidance and Options for Catholic Health Care and Unions* (Washington, D.C.: USCCB, 1999), p. 1.

32. *Respecting the Just Rights of Workers*, p. 1.

33. *Respecting the Just Rights of Workers*, p. 1.

34. *Respecting the Just Rights of Workers*, p. 13.

35. Pius XI, *Quadragesimo anno*, 79.

36. Pius XI, *Quadragesimo anno*, 80.

37. Paul VI, *Gaudium et spes*, 26.

38. Francis, *Laudato si'*, 156.

39. Alfred Lord Tennyson, "The Golden Year" in *The Collected Poems of Alfred Lord Tennyson* (Hertforshire: Wordsworth Editions Limited, 1994), p. 205.

40. Philip. K. Howard, *The Collapse of the Common Good: How America's Lawsuit Culture Undermines Our Freedom* (New York: Ballantine, 2001), p. 122.

41. Paul VI, *Gaudium et spes*, 26.

42. Francis, *Laudato si'*, 157.

43. Umesh Ramakrishnan, *There's No Elevator to the Top* (New York: Portfolio, 2008), p. 50.

44. Ramakrishnan, p. 50.

45. Justin Martyr, *First Apology*, 67.

46. John Mackey and Raj Sisodia, *Conscious Capitalism* (Boston: Harvard Business Review Press, 2014), pp. 247–248.

47. William J. Byron, SJ, *A Book of Quiet Prayer: For All the Seasons, Stages, Moods, and Circumstances of Life* (New York: Paulist Press, 2006), p. 131.

48. Hermann Hesse, *The Journey to the East*, trans. Hilda Rosner (New York: Picador, 2003), p. 34.

49. Robert K. Greenleaf, *Servant Leadership* (New York: Paulist Press, 1977), pp. 23–24.

50. Greenleaf, p. 147.

51. Greenleaf, p. 76.

52. Daniel Goleman, Richard Boyatzis, and Ann McKee, *Primal Leadership: Learning to Lead with Emotional Intelligence* (Boston: Harvard Business Review Press, 2004), p. 92.

53. "America's Business and Political Titans Face an Alienated Public. It's Time for Servant Leadership," *Houston Chronicle*, December 13, 2008, p. 8.

54. Larry C. Spears, ed., *Reflections on Leadership: How Robert Greenleaf's Theory of Servant Leadership Influenced Today's Top Management Thinkers* (New York: John Wiley & Sons,1995), pp. 4–7.

55. G. Richard Shell and Mario Moussa, *The Art of Woo: Using Strategic Persuasion to Sell Your Ideas* (New York: Penguin, 2007), p. 1.

56. Spears, p. 5.

57. John W. O'Malley, S.J., *The First Jesuits* (Cambridge: Harvard University Press, 1993), p. 72.

58. O'Malley, p. 73.

59. O'Malley, p. 73.

60. O'Malley, p. 73.

61. Pedro Arrupe, S.J., *One Jesuit's Spiritual Journey: Autobiographical Conversations with Jean-Claude Dietsch, S.J.* (St. Louis: Institute of Jesuit Sources, 1986), p. 74.

62. Robert F. Drinan, "The Melancholy Mood of English Catholics," *National Catholic Reporter*, September 24, 2004, Vol. 40, Issue 41, p. 19.

63. Drinan, p. 19.

64. Desmond Ryan, *The Catholic Parish: Institutional Discipline, Tribal Identity and Religious Development* (London: Sheed & Ward, 1996).

65. "Loneliness," *The Sunday Times Magazine,* May 27, 1962.

66. John W. Gardiner, "Uncritical Lovers, Unloving Critics," Commencement address given at Cornell University, Ithaca, NY, June 1, 1968. Published in *The Journal of Education Research*, Vol. 62, Issue 9 (May-June 1969), pp. 396–399.

67. John W. Gardiner, pp. 396–399.

68. John W. Gardiner, pp. 396–399.

69. Robert Goffee and Gareth Jones, "Why Should Anyone Be Led by You?" *Harvard Business Review*, (September–October 2000).

70. James J. Schiro, as quoted in Adam Bryant, "The C.E.O., Now Appearing on YouTube," *The New York Times*, Business Day, May 9, 2009. Accessed online at http://www.nytimes.com/2009/05/10/business/10corner.html?_r=0.

71. Thomas E. Ricks, *Fiasco: The American Military Adventure in Iraq,* 2003–2005 (New York: Penguin, 2006) p. 127.

72. John P. Kotter, *Leading Change* (Cambridge: Harvard Business Review Press, 2012).

73. Kotter, p. 59.

74. Kotter, p. 61.

75. Kotter, pp. 118–119.

76. Kotter, p. 135.

77. Kotter, p. 150.

78. Kotter, p. 150.

79. Kotter, p. 150.

80. Kotter, p. 150.

81. Kotter, p. 150.

82. David M. Herold and Donald B. Fedor, *Change the Way You Lead Change: Leadership Strategies that REALLY Work* (Stanford: Stanford University Press, 2008).

83. Herold and Fedor, p. 126.

84. Herold and Fedor, p. xiii.

85. Herold and Fedor, p. x.

86. Herold and Fedor, p. xi.

87. Herold and Fedor, p. xi.

88. Andrew Campbell and Stuart Sinclair, "The Crisis: Mobilizing boards for change," *McKinsey Quarterly*, February 2009. Access online at http://www.mckinsey.com/business-functions/organization/our-insights/the-crisis-mobilizing-boards-for-change.

89. Christine Haughney, "Fordham Seeks to Build on Manhattan Campus," *The New York Times*, January 22, 2009. Accessed at http://www.nytimes.com/2009/01/23/nyregion/23fordham.html.